GW00802402

Welcome to Ireland. The exit is over there.

Ireland through the eyes of an immigrant.

Brian Chama

Acknowledgements

Esther, thank you.

My heartfelt gratitude goes to Miriam, Ezekiel and Chinyanta for all the assistance.

I am indebted to the friends, acquaintances, colleagues and the good people of Ireland who made me feel so welcome.

I would also like to thank the folks who made my stay a challenge, because without you this story would not be possible. You taught me a lot about human nature and myself.

Contents

Fàilte: Irish. Welcome,

1 : to greet hospitably and with courtesy or cordiality

2 : to accept with pleasure the occurrence or presence of

Chapter 1

Another Non-National Has Landed

A new land, a new job and of course the prospect of being part of one of the most successful economies in the world, the Celtic Tiger, seemed like an opportunity too good to pass up. I arrived in Ireland at the beginning of 2001 with an overdose of enthusiasm. The romanticism of exploring the Emerald Isle, the land of a hundred thousand welcomes, having the craic, drinking Guinness in the land of its origin, throw in music and poetry, and there was no stopping me. The internet had painted such an irresistibly charming and rosy picture about it. Ireland, Ireeelaaand, here I come!

The flight from Johannesburg to London, via Vienna, was filled with the usual tedium of half-watched movies, a can or two of beer and the best cuisine on offer at twenty-one thousand feet. Trying to sleep comfortably in economy is an exercise in futility. I therefore had plenty of time to daydream about my mysterious destination and was worn out by the time I arrived at Heathrow airport. I emerged from the tunnels and corridors leading from the plane bleary eyed, exhausted and completely disoriented. "This must have been what a mole felt like when pulled out of the ground." Before I could complete the thought, I was confronted by the long winding immigration queues. I had not yet arrived!

"Which line should I join?"

This question had already been answered by the very clear signs above saying "EU Passports" and "All Other Passports", differentiating the queues according to nationalities. Just like the supermarket or toll bridge lines, it did not matter which one I joined, it would always end up being the slowest. In this case I could only watch in frustration as the "EU Passports" line, which as you would expect comprised EU passport holders only, sped forward while the rest of the world inched our way towards stern looking officials at a snail's pace.

This wait was followed by a humiliating interrogation by a very hostile immigration official, the gatekeeper to heaven. Eventually, she reluctantly stamped my passport. I had been given a whole of twenty-four hours in heaven.

My ordeal was far from over. Before the next leg of my flight, from London to Dublin, I decided to go and confirm if my luggage had been checked through to Dublin. The Aer Lingus staff, Ireland's national airline, told me that they had not received it from British Airways yet. I went to the BA desk where I was told that they had passed it on. I was shunted between the two desks three times or so. The Aer Lingus desk staff seemed to enjoy this game as they kept laughing every time I was ping-ponged between the two desks. They eventually tired of their game and told me that they were on strike that day, and that I would only get my luggage after a couple of days or so. I on the other hand was tired, anxious and not in the least amused.

Arriving in Dublin was an altogether different matter. The immigration officer was friendly. He greeted me pleasantly as I handed him my passport.

"First time to Ireland?"

"Yes it is."

"What brings you to Ireland? "

"Work."

He leafed through my passport, took a close look at my visa, stamped it and handed the passport back.

"Welcome to Ireland. You'll need to report to the Galway Garda Síochána within two weeks."

He waved me through. It was by far the best immigration experience of my life.

On another trip a few years later, I noticed that things had reverted to normal, the other normal that is, hostile and humiliating.

It was on to baggage collection. No bags for me, apart from my hand luggage. I completed the lost luggage form and proceeded to the arrivals lounge. At that time, Dublin airport was still a nondescript structure that seemed to have been randomly cobbled together, not making any statement to the world, just an airport. Fly in, fly out.

Not knowing that I could have taken a bus or train to Galway, I went to the check-in desk to confirm the flight for the last leg of my journey. The travel agent back home had not heard of Galway before. Nor had I. But all roads led to Galway. I confirmed my flight and dragged my tired body down to the airport pub. Oh, how I needed a rest!

When I ordered my first pint of Guinness, I almost yanked it out of the barman's hand before the customary pause, leaving it to settle, then the last pouring, followed by the final pause before taking the first sip. I did not wait for the final settling. The barman smiled knowingly. I had just messed up my initiation into the Guinness drinking ritual.

Shortly, an Irishman came and sat next to me at the counter.
"Where did you fly from?"
"Where are you going?"
"What do you do?"

He bought me the next pint and made more small talk as we drained the pints. He turned down my offer to buy him the next one, wished me well, bid me goodbye and left.

I was astounded. The immigration officer was pleasant, the barman was friendly and other patrons were friendly too. Shocking! The land of a hundred thousand welcomes indeed. I got two more pints of the black stuff and made my way to the check-in desk and subsequent departure for the unknown, the city of Galway.

It was a turbulent flight in a small propeller plane. Looking down below, I was surprised at how all the land seemed to have been completely partitioned. Literally every single space was demarcated by lines of walls or trees. Every inch had been claimed.

If Dublin airport was shabby and drab, Galway airport turned out to be an even smaller and shabbier clearing by the sea. An old man offloaded the bags. Someone joked that he also performed the customs and immigration duties. Where on earth was this? Had I just found the middle of nowhere?

A taxi booked by my host company was waiting for me. The driver was a pleasant and chatty man. He was surprised to see that I only had a small piece of hand luggage with me. It was all that was required to jumpstart the small talk. As he drove me to the hotel, he gave me a survival tip that I thought to be useless at the time. "When you hear people making stupid remarks, just ignore them. They are uneducated and ignorant. Just ignore them." He said.

When visiting other places before, I had been warned about certain streets or parts of town to avoid. Do not drop off at this or that station on the Metro in Washington, stay away from Little Haiti in Miami, if you want to live to a ripe old age. Avoid Hillbrow when in Johannesburg, do not enter the favelas in Rio, or avoid Kidbrooke at all costs from a Londoner.

Unfortunately, just like in the proverbial "do not press the red button" situation, such warnings only served to heighten my curiosity and foster an inexplicable sense of adventure. No one had ever given me such a warning and in such a situation before. I was struggling to understand his accent and I had no clue what he was talking about. So I decided to ignore his warning instead.

For a while afterwards, I did struggle with understanding the Irish accent in general. They also struggled to understand me. Eventually, I tuned into the local accents and jargon and overcame this crucial huddle.

The following morning, I walked the streets of Galway wondering where everybody had gone. The streets were empty. I could see an odd couple here, an old man or woman slowly walking over there but no one else. It was in the thick of winter. The cold made me realise how ill-attired I was. I quickly got a coat. I also needed to get a change of clothes, fast. My luggage was taking longer than two days.

After doing more shopping, I wandered around aimlessly. I still saw very few people around.

Then I stepped into a pub. This is where everyone was, where life in Ireland revolved, around the famous Irish pub. It had a low ceiling, wooden furniture with maroon or green upholstery, interesting décor too, not the mass produced prints. They certainly had character. This was before the sanitized and aluminum furnished mega pubs flooded the place.

As it turned out, Galway was a charming town or city as the locals insisted. It had an array of entertainment, a university, a number of colleges, and a history to match. Big acts in music, cinema and politics would show up. Mandela visited. The gentleman who brought Barings Bank down, the oldest UK merchant bank (it used to be anyway), made Galway his home. It attracted all sorts.

The loud sound of people talking and laughing took me aback as I opened the door to step in. It had been so quiet just a few inches outside the door. There were lots of people crammed into a seemingly tiny space, men and women, with a cloud of cigarette smoke hanging above, menacingly watching over the proceedings. It was before the smoking ban.

Every visit to a pub or club warranted another one to the laundry. Whatever I had been wearing had to go into the washing machine. Everything would acquire that revolting, stale stench of cigarette smoke the morning after. My hair would smell too, especially since I had an afro then. It was disgusting. For the greater good of having fun, the health implications were shunted to one side.

It all started in a land very far away from here, when the Celtic circus roared into town. I was minding my own business in South Africa when a friend excitedly told me about the road shows, the job fairs being held by Irish companies in the affluent suburb of Sandton.

Watching traditional music inside one of the oldest pubs in Athlone

One evening I dragged a Zulu colleague along, to go and see for ourselves what the hoo-ha was all about.

Bank of Ireland, Sun Microsystems, Andersen Consulting (then), you name them, most of the big technology hitters that had set up shop in Ireland at that time were represented. Boy, were they eager to snap up the best talent South Africa had to offer! I felt a shade of discomfort when interacting with some of the agents. The impression I got was that they may have been looking for *White* South African talent only. I hastily brushed such retrogressive thoughts aside, putting my apprehension down to the time spent dealing with some Boers who were still reeling from ages of Apartheid indoctrination. That is a story for another day.

I wholeheartedly immersed myself into finding out what was on offer, who was involved and what they did. A CV dropped here, a phone number or email address written down there, and a brochure snapped up from over there. I was impressed with what I saw and heard. My excitement went through the roof, closely followed by my expectations.

My Zulu friend travelled to Ireland in November for his interview. He promptly turned down the job offer when he returned to South Africa. "My friend, it is very cold and there are no Black people." He replied when I asked him why.

This answer made me laugh. I concluded that his timidity was probably down to naivety and a lack of exposure, this being his first time to travel beyond the borders of South Africa. Not me, nothing can put me off. After all I had been to the States a number of times, the UK and a number of African countries. Ireland, bring it on! I mentally gave myself a big pat on the back for being more adventurous, open minded and better travelled than my Zulu friend.

Recently my car had been stolen. Dealing with some racist or xenophobic locals had become tiresome. It was time to try something different. I received three job offers and duly accepted one from a US company that had just established a branch in Ireland.

Companies had swooped on Ireland to take advantage of the prevailing favourable business environment.

I handed in my resignation and applied for the recently introduced work visa. Mine was the very first such visa issued by the embassy in my home country.

My prior dealings with embassy staff usually involved relatively junior to mid-ranking officials. This time the ambassador came out to chat with me. He interrogated me about my professional qualifications, work experience and details about how I had been offered the job. He made a few grunts, seemingly unconvinced, but disappeared to grudgingly, I thought, approve my permission to work in Ireland.

When I got to Ireland I had to report and register all my details at a local police station. This process was repeated each time the visa came up for renewal. A new visa would be affixed in the passport, and then it was on to presenting myself at a local police station to be registered or reregistered, and my passport stamped. A new "Certificate of Registration" would then be issued. It had my photo, all vital identifying information and a biometric chip. For some inexplicable reason that I never bothered to find out it was labeled: "This is not an identity card."

This process was also repeated whenever I moved from one town to another. There was a fee levied for the process each time. I wondered what registration method criminals went through.

Renewing the visa was quite an experience. First, there was the early morning trip to Dublin. I am talking 04:00 A.M. Other immigrant souls would already be in a queue, standing, and waiting on the street. Sometimes it would be raining. At other times the full force of the winter might be around to keep us company. If you look closely enough on the pavement along Burgh Quay, the street that runs along Dublin Canal (be careful, there could be drug addicts on the inner walkway, they were a bit scary but generally harmless), you will find my dignity lying right there on the pavement, where I left it.

The offices opened around 09:00 A.M. There would be a bit of excitement as it would spur a mad dash for the all important number tags. At this stage being indoors and able to sit down would provide some sort of comfort. To be followed by more waiting. Some of which time would be spent watching and trying to guess other applicants' life stories using only what they were wearing and the shape of the forehead as clues. Listening to other applicants being grilled by the officials provided an additional way to pass the time. There was always an audience comprising other immigrants watching and listening to every person's supplications attentively, but indifferently. You became oblivious to this audience as soon as your number was called, and you went onto the stage for a performance that would determine your continued presence in heaven or subsequent ejection. Watching paint dry would have equally been entertaining.

I would snap out of the self hypnosis when the number on my tag was called. Reprieve would only be guaranteed once I reached the counter and submitted a life story which satisfied the immigration official.

Applicants were treated not as guests but pests or parasites to be discouraged and humiliated into thinking twice before lodging that visa application. That is what my observations and experiences told me.

When I went back to Africa to apply for another visa, the attitude of the officers had not changed. One embassy official who appeared to be in his early thirties was quite brash, condescending, and downright rude. At another time, I again had the misfortune to find myself dealing with the Embassy in London. A lady who was handling my application literally blasted my ears and face away. I felt like a small boy in front of the Headmaster all over again. The language she used was undiplomatic, to put it mildly. If I had not needed to travel to Dublin then, I would have withdrawn my application then, but I had to humble myself. Diplomats turned out to be an oxymoron in these confines.

After I had lived in Ireland for over eight years, I decided to apply for some kind of residency permit. It was a humiliating, frustrating and murky process. They had something called a long term residence permit whose purpose was not clearly defined. I had to wait for two more years after submitting the initial application. Each time I called immigration to ask about the procedure, how to go about it or the status of my application, I got a completely different story. Every single time, without fail! Was it old fashioned incompetence or just deliberate obfuscation? I did not hang around long enough to find out.

It started to irritate me when a colleague whined, complained and worried about her 'papers'. Finally the penny dropped. I realized why she had to go and schmooze or plead with a local TD to intervene in the processing of her application.

Funny enough, an immigration officer asked me one time why I had not applied for an Irish passport after having worked in Ireland for over eight years. I thought he would or should know seeing as some former officers had set up immigration consultancies to handhold the immigrants through an opaque application process that resembled a maze. There was a fee involved of course.

Chapter 2

In the Mist of the Celtic Tiger

Once upon a time, Ireland was just like any third world country. Taxes were high, the politicians were corrupt, families huge, poverty was endemic, and the economy was mostly agrarian. Donkeys, no – horses and cows - delivered vegetables and fruit into town each morning. Apparently, people were less greedy, less materialistic and generally kind to each other. They went to mass every Sunday and the Catholic Church ruled supreme. They were also nice to foreigners. There were no foreigners to speak of. Such is what an old Irish sage told me.

People were happy and content.

No, they weren't!

They scampered in different directions, to all ends of the world to find or set up better lives for themselves. Some went as far as the United States. The number of undocumented Irish immigrants in the States was significant enough for the Irish government to try and lobby the White House on their behalf. When the immigration issue flared up in the States, mainly sparked by their neighbour on the southern border, Mexico, Irish illegals got caught up in the kerfuffle. They needed to look for solutions. Wink, wink, nudge, nudge. They were not from Mexico.

Others only went as far as Britain. One legacy being that there is a big Irish community of people who emigrated in their own right and the descendants of immigrants. I also met a good number of Irish people whose parents or other relatives had worked in the mines, hospitals, schools and churches in Africa.

The old man I was chatting with had just returned from Australia.

In the meantime the mother-island, after years of trying, was finally allowed into the exclusive club of the European Union. At the stroke of a pen access to half a billion consumers was granted. Irish industry could sell to them. There was access to Europe wide expertise. Business people, shoppers, workers, holiday makers, students, politicians, and criminals could now conduct their affairs without too many barriers or restrictions. Farmers could avail of the popular but infamous subsidy. The EU money taps were opened up literally catapulted the country into the first world.

A term normally associated with the high growth economies in South East Asia was used to describe the exploding Irish economy. The Celtic Tiger, it was called. It was born with a full set of teeth and an appetite to match.

Overnight, the menial and farming based economy had been transformed. It was now an advanced economy with a huge demand for highly skilled workers. The political, economic and social rhetoric evolved accordingly. The knowledge economy was here to stay.

Having gained access to the EU market, Ireland set about taking full advantage of all that the EU membership had to offer. In addition to being a net recipient of EU funding, they knocked down the corporate tax which lured multinational conglomerates to Ireland. Tax was just one, among many incentives. Foreign direct investments poured in. Some EU countries were infuriated.

The Irish put this success down to excellent planning, an educated workforce and English being the official language. As people's incomes rose, so did the demand. Demand for nice houses, new ones. Nice cars, new ones too.

At first uninvited but later accommodated, Jo Foreigner came to the party too. Jo also needed a place to stay and a way to get around. So lots of cars were sold. Lots of houses were built and sold.

There was no satisfying the demand for rental accommodation. Unsecured loans were handed out. Mortgages were dished out. Ninety percent, ninety five percent mortgages were being offered. I thought that was high. Then it went up to one hundred and ten percent.

The developers profited, the bankers made money, and the investors cashed in. Speculators also got their cut. For the less ambitious, there were lots of jobs to be had in the sector. The government got its VAT, taxes, stamp duty and statistics. A lot of fantastic statistics. There was money to be made, political capital to be mopped up, and elections to be won.

There was also The Bubble to be inflated.

The country was flush with money. The people were flush with money. Money, lots of money, not cash. Both did what the proverbial sailor does, albeit, whilst under the influence. They spent it. On luxury and vanity projects.

They have the Washington monument in Washington D.C, the Eiffel tower in Paris, Big Ben in London, well, here comes the Dublin Spire. A tall mass of steel smack in the centre of Dublin, giving the finger to anyone who dared say, dared think even that Ireland was small or only famous for Guinness. How much will it cost to build and keep this thing shiny? Who cares! Lansdowne road stadium is looking tired, it was knocked down and a state of the art stadium built in its place. Vanity projects found themselves at the forefront of national priorities and won the day.

Almost every town found the need to commemorate its own heroes. If it did not have any hero worth the distinction, it simply expropriated one or made something up.

All sorts of sculptures and things, lots of things, littered the sides of roads and motorways, bearing witness and paying homage to the tiger times. The countryside and most places outside the Pale came late to the party. But they joined in with admirable fervour.

Houses in the rural and remote areas which everyone had shunned were subsidized with a tax exemption (I think it was called Section 23) to encourage people to buy there.

The Irish language was compulsory in early education but of no functional value beyond that. All teachers and students had to pass the exam. A lot of money was spent on preserving Gaeltacht areas and on the production of programming and maintenance of a radio and TV channels in the Irish language.

Watch out for the Spire if you are flying over O'Connell Street in Dublin. It is pointy at the top.

Sponge Bob could now speak Irish, this among many imported TV programs. I thought there was better imported programming on TG4, the local Irish language TV channel than the English ones. All signs and government literature had to be produced or rewritten in two languages, English and Irish. One local authority failed to get rid of any of the Irish pamphlets even though they were obliged to produce them, just in case. The EU was lobbied to give the Irish language official status. Meetings at The Hague or wherever the EU functionaries sat could now be translated into Irish, live. Was it worth every penny?

You could now sit and have a chat with Oscar, right there on Shop Street in Galway. Was he born here, or did he die here? Maybe he visited? I do not know whose bag that is.

The Irish civil service became bloated and was reputed to be one of, if not the highest paying in Europe. Politicians were flying all over the place to solicit for foreign investment and sell the story of Ireland. You would be hard pressed to find a top government official celebrating St. Patrick's day in Ireland. They all jetted off to New York, Sydney and London to "officiate" at the parades. Were they footing their own bill? Anyone who dared raise an eyebrow, let alone object would be rounded on, shouted down and quickly put in their place. They were then lectured on the need to do away with the "small Ireland mentality".

The citizens also went on a spending spree. They collected cars, paintings, holidays abroad, and weekend shopping trips to New York. It was rumoured to be cheaper than shopping in Dublin. Plane ticket, hotel room and entertainment included! The taxman grimaced at the loss of VAT revenue and undeclared customs duties.

There was an interesting spectacle at the start of every year of people scrambling to register the latest car models with that specific year's number. The year of registration would move up with the start of the new year to 04, 05, and so on. So any new vehicle registered in the New Year will have that year's number. In January being seen in a car with the latest year's registration was kind of fashionable. The more the number of luxury cars to a family, the higher the status.

Cars were not the only thing that pre-occupied people with spending money they did not have. Houses were the next big thing. Every person wanted to own a house. No, that did not sound right. Everybody wanted to invest in property. Developers, solicitors, estate agents, and other middlemen buzzing around were now the men about town. By the way, did I mention that it was all financed by loans?

There were new developments everywhere. In areas of high demand, people would camp in queues before the properties went on sale. Similar to the way people camp and queue up for concert tickets. Sleeping bags, coffee mugs, the whole hyped look. If they were lucky enough to get to the front of the queue, they would then hand over four thousand euro or more to the developer to get on the list. Yes that is four thousand euro or more of their hard earned or fictitious money! The security deposit was supposed to be refundable. But sometimes it would be used to secure the reservation.

For properties bought off plan, the expectation was that the value of the property would explode by the time a single brick was

21

laid. And they did. The successful punters, or buyers, would then walk into the nearest bank and apply for a deposit free mortgage on the house. Some built up portfolios of property by stacking them up in a chain of debt. Borrowing against one property to buy another one for the lucrative rental and capital markets. Housing estates popped up everywhere. It was as if they had been designed by the same person. Every estate was the same. Every town started looking even more like the next town.

Most of these houses were quite uninspired. They generally had two, three or rarely four bedrooms. Finding a semi-detached meant paying more. Being at a corner meant an extra twenty square feet of grass. Add an extra ten or twenty thousand for the privilege. If it was connected and setup for gas heating and cooking, that will be an extra three thousand please, the agent would say with a shifty look in his eyes. That was until the gas prices skyrocketed. Gas was not such a strong selling point anymore.

As with all goods or services in high demand, the quality of the houses being churned out started suffering from the poor or rushed workmanship syndrome. Leaking roofs and plumb work, creaking stairs, badly laid tiles, poorly finished carpentry work became common. Snag lists the length of an adult's arm became the norm.

I tried to jump onto the bandwagon, but fell off in horror at what I saw. My spanned the big city, medium sized and small commuter towns, down to the villages The Tiger had barely touched. My search for a dream home took to Dublin, Galway, Athlone, Moate, Kilbeggan, Enfield, Mullingar, Ballymahon, and Edgeworthstown to mention only a few places. The script was the same. Stacks of similar looking estates, no matter where I went it looked like a trip to the bread section of a supermarket. Except that instead of stacks of loaves of bread, it was dull, uninspiring estates comprising rows upon rows of houses. One would have expected them to be cheap, but they were not. The long queues of anxious and excited buyers coupled with smug looking builders handing out glossy brochures to accompany the shiny, well presented and exquisitely decorated show houses at jaw dropping prices. If you scratched beneath the surface just a little bit, the façade was quickly exposed. Poor quality or rushed workmanship, and cheap materials. And too expensive!

Britain did not matter to the Irish economy any more. Some of the phrases I heard bandied about included how "We [they] do not have to jump when England sneezed" and "Economically and politically punching above our [their] weight." There was a big push to boost more trade and cultural ties with Europe and the United States.

In addition to the now unquenchable desire to preserve all things ancient, people became fervent collectors or investors in art. Interest was high in pieces done by Irish artists.

There was a lot of bickering about how or even whether to preserve any area with a whiff of buried Celtic archeological artifacts. The rampant construction of new motorways fueled the debate. Money was allocated and experts hired to survey, excavate or dig the sites before construction started. I met and spoke with one such team. They had come from the UK to excavate and take images of the ground beneath the hills of Tara. Archeological treasures had been discovered by people digging randomly in the bog.

There was a surge of pride when names like the Quinns made it onto The Times' rich list for a few years.

The Cranes and the Celtic Tiger in full swing. Never mind the swans, that piece of land used to be a dump. Now it was a prime plot. Do not take a close look at the water. How many apartments were sold?

Irish people who had escaped the hardships to the US and other countries started returning. There was talk of resettling or helping Irish people who had become destitute in the UK. Long gone emigrants started to return.

It definitely made business sense to set up a presence in Ireland and export to the rest of Europe without paying higher tax rates to the Germans and the French. However, the infrastructure left much to be desired. If we needed something delivered urgently, sometimes it had to be diverted to Shannon airport and then delivered by road to Galway. It took less time to fly from Düsseldorf in Germany to Dublin than travelling by bus, car or train from Dublin to Galway.

Construction sites everywhere!

Driving on the narrow winding roads was a nightmare. The roads seemed to have had no plan whatsoever. One person jokingly told me that the roads were just built along the trails the sheep used. It was easier. The effect was to find yourself breathlessly inching towards your destination on a narrow, hilly and randomly winding strip. It required faith.

That's right, apartments, hotels, everything, going up everywhere. Even on the other side of the river.

Dun Laoghaire, right on the nose of Dublin, pronounced something like "Doon Lorrey". I never could get it right, but can you spot them?

If you were unfortunate enough to find yourself behind a tractor or other slow moving vehicle, it would add an extra thirty minutes or more to the journey. For some strange reason I usually found myself stuck behind a fast car driven at twenty miles per hour. Potholes and the rough uneven surface further added to the challenge. Such depressing circumstances were compounded by the inconvenience of having to pass through small towns and villages like Kilbeggan, Ballinasloe, Kinnegad, or Moate that were dotted along the way just to annoy you. It felt like there were hundreds of them.

To preserve or not to preserve, that is the million euro question.

Traffic slowed to a crawl when you reached the perimeter of these villages. No matter how much you stretched your neck, it was impossible to see what was happening up front due to the said meandering nature of the road. It was as if someone evil had deliberately designed them that way to test how long a person's patience would last before they snapped and ripped their own head off in frustration.

The narrowness of the roads was such that when you met an oncoming truck or bus, you just had to close your eyes, grit your teeth and pray that you will still be in one piece when you get to the other side. There was no hard shoulder to escape onto. In fact most of the roads had stone walls built along them. Stone walls. Houses were also built just inches from the road. Is it not dangerous to step right into the road from such a main door? I never heard of any fatality under such circumstances. A friend, whilst driving from Galway to Ballina climbed one such wall. Yes, using her car. An oncoming truck was unwilling to share the narrow road.

When driving in city centres such as Dublin, Limerick, or Cork, the random road arrangement threw me off track on lots of occasions. I would have plotted a seemingly straight forward route to my destination. Then it would all spiral out of control the moment I missed one turn. Making a relatively safe and logical assumption that if I just kept going straight on, I would be able to double back onto my original route. It never worked. The road would go off on a complete tangent, usually morph into a one way street and before I could say "I am lost" I would have veered miles off track. Usually you "go round in circles" when lost. Not here. I would end up anywhere, never seeing the same landmark twice. I soon learned that if I took a wrong turn, it was best to stop and plan the trip from scratch.

If you thought that was enough, then you had to wait until you reached a junction. The road signs were interesting. They would be non-existent for most of the trip and then I would come to a junction that had hundreds of road signs, no, 'sign-lets', pointing everywhere. If I was fortunate enough to be alone on the road then I would read through them at my leisure and then take the correct turn. If on the other hand there were cars behind me, car horns would hurry me through the process increasing the chances of having to make a U-turn further down the road.

Beautiful flowers on the stone wall along the road. The tractor is doing its thing, watch out for that house, and yes, that river is called Suck.

An East African friend, Ogli and I drove to Kilkenny for the Kilkenny Comedy Festival. We did not want to risk losing our way by using the unfamiliar country roads, so we went all the way through Dublin, the long way around. We stuck to the main roads and towns that we knew well and ended up wasting most of the day on the road.

On our way back, in the early hours of the morning, we decided to bet the house on the relatively shorter country roads. Every so often, Ogli would stare in my face to make sure that I had not dozed off. We knew only too well that any slight batting of my eyelids would be punished by a collision with the stone wall.

Where are you headed? You have seven seconds to find your destination. Look out for oncoming traffic by the way. The dark door and window outlines were green for The Fiddlers and orange for The Tea Ju-something - plus the white background, it's the flag!

We were woken from this little get home safely routine when we came across a police car that was weaving from one side of the road to the other. It had all the colours, markings, and lights. It appeared to be a drunken Garda literally staggering home in an official police car. I waited until he had staggered all the way to one side of the road before speeding past. It took us about twenty minutes to pass that car. There had been a big truck backed up behind me.

Good luck to him or her. Ogli stopped staring in my face for the rest of the way.

There were numerous road accidents in Ireland at that time. This was put down to the poor state of the roads, the prevalence of drink driving exacerbated by a poor public transport system. Boy racers were also mentioned. Someone else mumbled something about drugs. There were some murmurs about the high number of learner drivers on the roads. People would get their first provisional licence, attempt and fail the test and continue renewing and driving on provisional licences for the next five years. I had to repeat the driving test to get the Irish driving licence. I did not wait for five years.

Someone found a way to pull Jo Foreigner into the debate and apportioned Jo a big chunk of the blame for this phenomenon. Apparently, the influx of poor drivers from abroad had contributed to the carnage on the roads. A penalty points system and random breath tests were introduced. They hardly made a dent on the number of fatalities.

Public transport in the country side remained non-existent. After an evening out I would typically wait in line at the taxi rank for a taxi home. There were no buses available at that time. And wait I would. Ending up soaked to the skin and sobering up in the process because of the rained. Most times I would give up on waiting and walk. This would take a good forty five minutes. Reaching the house soaked to the skin and sober. I bought a couple of umbrellas that got blown apart literally the first time I used them. The rainproof coat worked better but lobbing it around was a chore. What a price to pay for a bit of pleasure and a lot of grief.

At one time in Galway, I stayed near a pub. It was a popular, out of town kind of place. As such if you observed the pub's car park, it would be full of cars as the evening went on. Check back early in the morning, and there will only be two or three cars remaining. What happened to the others? Did they all have designated drivers? I once saw a man with his friend stagger back to their car. The chap who was meant to drive fumbled with the key before finally opening the door, getting in and driving off. In full view of everyone.

With a financial injection from the EU, the public transport network expanded. As part of the National Development Plan, motorways were built left, right and centre. Some semblance of sanity was finally brought to the duration of journeys and the actual travelling experience. You had to give some allowance for the strange driving habits of people who had never driven on motorways before and others who thought them to be racing tracks.

A lot of noise was made in protest because the building of motorways led to the villages and small towns being bypassed. They moaned about the negative impact to local businesses. Did no one care what the insanity of a possible two hour journey taking twice that long could be doing to the economy?

The Government tried to milk as much credit as it could. Signs went up along these roads stating that part of the money for the projects had been splashed out by the EU. Was it was a response meant to debunk some government claims?

Projects would be launched with much fanfare. After a while the waste or lack of foresight would become evident.

The Dublin tunnel that was meant to divert heavy goods vehicles, super trucks, from the street roads was found to have been under dimensioned. The super trucks will not be able to fit in it. A new rail track was built at a huge cost to service a small village. After all the work had been completed, only a small number of passengers actually used the service. The Bridge to Nowhere was now in good company.

A small bus stop between Nenagh and Limerick had a beautiful fountain complete with flowers and stones. There was no bus shelter in sight. At least people could enjoy the view while getting waiting. Never mind the rain.

There was a feeder road adjoining the newly constructed motorway close to where I lived. That small road was dug up almost every three months. Workmen would arrive in their small truck, a tractor and some shovels. They would dig the road up and lay some stones and tar. It usually took them a couple of weeks or so. They would then finish it off using small hand driven compactors. The road was used by big trucks to make deliveries into the town. Needless to say it would be full of potholes within a few weeks. This was repeated at least three times. Finally, someone saw sense and decided to hire a decent road builder.

A local council in one city met and re-classified as commercial, a piece of land that was in the path of a proposed motorway. This was shortly before the new motorway project was announced. Commercial land attracted a higher rate under the compensation scheme. The minister responsible reprimanded the council and directed them to reverse the decision.

The planning permission process had become questionable. Tribunals were established to look into the matter and to clean up the processes, among others issues. They sat for years. Some joked that a tribunal needed to be set up to look into the prevalence of tribunals.

Every so often someone from an important sounding department would go round testing the drinking water around the country. In Galway they found some undesirable bacteria normally found in human and animal excrement. A "Boil your water before drinking it" alert was beamed out. This happened so many times that I resorted to drinking only bottled water.

My travels around the country confirmed the origin of the term "The Emerald Isle". It was a very green country. Mostly due to the rain. It rains a lot.

The EU shamelessly takes its share of the credit for financing this road using the bottom half of the huge sign. The signs are bilingual. Watch out for the wall as you accelerate to 100, but slow down if you are not so about where you're going.

The reference to the emeralds had nothing to do with an abundance of precious stones or natural resources. It was due to the abundance of grass. Lots of green grass all the year round. If the sunny days persisted for a few days it would be the talk of the country. Temperature records would be mentioned. Old not so fashionable holiday shorts, shirts or skirts would be dusted off and put on display, all sorts of bodies that is.

There was one sign for 'Silver mines' along a road to Limerick, I was not sure if it was operational. Other than that there are no natural resources to speak of. It took me a while to realize how little by way of natural resources this country had.

34

One big resource that was in abundant supply was "The gift of the gab" as it was called. That is the gift of talking. There was even a rock somewhere near Cork rumored and believed to have the ability to give the pilgrim a top up of the gift of the gab if they ran out. That's one thing people did a lot of. Talk. There are several such places of pilgrimage or monuments in Ireland. You could climb Croagh Patrick mountain and be frisked for everything from water to parking. Quite apt as it was supposedly climbed by the saint who supposedly took money for some rites and kept some for himself.

No one wanted the pipeline for gas that had been languishing off the coast of Mayo (or Clare) to pass in their backyard. There was lot of fighting between the company and activists. Would it have made a dent in the world supplies?

Someone, please show me where that pot of gold is hidden.

The Celtic Tiger was one big party which was not going to end and where no one knew or cared who was paying. Some good things were done, mistakes made and a lot of waste incurred. Was it a squandered opportunity? People's attitudes hardened. Now that the money was here, a servile class was needed to toil for some crumbs.

A Berber friend summed it up thus: "Getting the priorities right when you are rolling in the money is hard. Buying style is even harder."

Between Connemara and Cliften on the Emerald Isle. Near the Gaeltacht.

Still somewhere on the Emerald Isle. The Gaeltacht and the bog are still nearby.

Somewhere else on the Emerald Isle, not far from Cork. The land was very green and yes, well partitioned.

Chapter 3

Shelter is a Human Need

There was a lot of pushing and shoving as I slowly crept forward in the crowd. Every minute someone would push past me, heading in the opposite direction, the broad smile on their face accompanied by a triumphant look in the eyes. One hand would be clutching the prize tightly. They had just got their hands on the all important Galway Advertiser! Only the accommodations insert. I would look at them enviously but still be happy to squeeze my way forward and fill the pocket of air they had just vacated. Within fifteen to twenty minutes the scramble would be gone, the crowd dispersed. These guys had as much claim to inventing the flash mob as anybody. Afterwards, a number of people would be standing, sitting, or walking up and down Shop Street, poring over the paper, looking at the adverts for apartments, rooms, houses or flats that were being let that week.

It was critical to be at that newspaper's office in time to get a copy of the accommodations supplement. It was a weekly paper. Missing a week was not an option. Competition was stiff as students, professionals, workers and drifters would all be jostling for a place to stay in the city.

I finally got myself a copy! There was no time to fluff about or admire the view, phone calls needed to be made to would be landlords to arrange viewings and possible lettings. To my horror, every single landlord I called told me that the flat or room had already been taken. I went through the same process the following week with absolutely no luck. Someone told me that my accent was a dead giveaway, and that most landlords had the powers to sift through prospective tenants just from the way they spoke. In the third week I finally got one viewing. It was a small bedsit. I had a quick look, asked how much the rent was and declared there and then that I was in love with the place (I was not) and would take it. To my surprise, the landlord looked at me suspiciously and told me that there were other people coming to see it and that he would call me back later. He never did.

By this time I was getting desperate. At this point the bed and breakfast I was staying at was becoming too expensive, monotonous and inconvenient. The rooms were cramped and I could not even boil an egg. I needed to move.

It was the fourth week. Maybe my fortunes would change this time. I performed the same ritual again. Got back in the queue, made a number of frantic phone calls and I finally struck gold.

It was a room in a four bedroom house, in one of the more "interesting" parts of Galway to live. It was in a housing estate close to the Westside. There were three other occupants in the house. I paid the landlady the deposit and two weeks' worth of rent and promptly moved my stuff in. The B & B owner, who seemed like a nice man actually drove me there. He was not impressed with my new abode. I was not sure whether it was because of something he knew about that place or the loss of a long term lodger.

Later in the evening the other occupants came back from work. They were in dirty boots and messy clothes, all manual labourers. I introduced myself and made a bit of small talk.

It went downhill from then on.

What a ramshackle of a house it was. Paint was peeling off the walls, it was cold, and it leaked. Everything was dilapidated, it was a nightmare. To make matters worse, my Irish housemates usually came back late at night, drunk, and started playing music very loudly into the early hours of the morning. To get any amount of sleep, I would have to get up, walk up the stairs and tell them to tone it down. They always acted surprised, apologised and turned the volume of the music down. We repeated this routine almost every other night of the working week.

The kitchen was like a war zone. A bulldozer was required to clear out the garbage to make a path to the stove. Then some kind of bio-hazard SWAT team would be required to disinfect the place before even thinking of frying an egg in there. There was a whole ecosystem in the fridge. Things were growing on what might have been food at some point in time but had been left in the fridge for months on end. I tried to clean up a few times but stood no chance. I was always fighting a losing battle. It only served to reinvigorate them. It was almost like I was challenging them to a garbage dumping fight. No one else seemed to care or even bothered.

To get from one end of the lounge to the other you needed a pole vault. There were clothes on the floor and plates of half eaten dinners. There were boxes of left-over take-aways, beer bottles and cans. You name it, if it belonged in the rubbish bin, you would find it there. I never spent any time in the lounge.

These folks rarely bathed. I saw or heard them come and go most days. I rarely heard the shower nor saw them go in there especially after work considering the heavy manual work they did.

When going out on Thursday or Friday evenings however, they would pop out of their rooms looking all spruced up, hair greasy with gel, and looking really smart. I would not have heard a single drop of water hit the floor. How did that happen?

I refuse to talk about the toilet.

A Spanish colleague I worked with wanted to come and see the new place I had moved into. I prevaricated and dilly-dallied, then gave him every single excuse under the sun until he finally gave up. It was embarrassing.

It got worse.

One night, they started shouting abuse from their room after I had asked them to reduce the volume of their rock music. "F**k this, f**k that, f**king n****r, Black c**t" and so it went on. It went on and on and on. I do not know whether they thought I could not hear them. It was horrible.

I remember being in the kitchen the following morning when one of them walked in. I was cutting some bread or something for my breakfast. He cheerily blurted out a greeting and made a beeline for the fridge. When there was no reply from me, he looked around and up from the fridge.

Did he really expect me to chat and smile at him? But he did see the look on my face and the knife in my hand. There was no need for words. He quickly dashed out of the kitchen.

It was quiet for the next few days. We did not talk. By then, I had given the landlady notice and was all packed. I did not even say bye when I left. The landlady was not very pleased that her most reliable tenant was leaving after only a few weeks. Apparently I was the only one who always paid the rent on time. She tried to cajole me into staying, it did not work. She held on to my deposit for a few weeks. Only by persistently hounding her did I get my money back.

Meantime, it was back to the Galway Advertiser, through which I found a new place to stay, in an area called Newcastle. It was a relatively better place and much closer to the business park where I worked. It was also a four bed-roomed house, well maintained and as such in a much better shape than the previous dump. It was certainly warmer. Two professionals and a student shared the house. They seemed a nicer and friendlier bunch. They took my deposit and I moved in.

As it turned out, the owner of the property was an old lady whose son was a TD and a minister in the government. I learned this later. Anyhow, she was furious when she came round and realized that her agents had sublet the remaining room to a Black person. She

41

pulled one of them outside for a chat. He came back and bluntly told me that Ms Monaghan did not like me. But I had only met her, I thought. Meeting was not even the word to describe the encounter. She had only seen me then for the first time. I was dumbfounded, but I stayed. The memories from the previous hellhole were still fresh. Anything would now be a palace, a breath of air (the air did not even need to be fresh) and in all reality a giant step for mankind's peace of mind. My peace of mind that is.

The view from my bedroom window. A housemate returns from work. My cotton slacks and shirts, thin shoes, and silk socks were no match for the cold.

The conversation in the house was intelligent and mature. We talked politics, sport and culture. We debated the issues of the day such as the Iraq war, which they supported and I thought was wrong.

There was courtesy towards each other and respect for each others' space.

They were curious about the food I ate and how I cooked it. I was unimpressed with their cuisine and diet in general. We laughed about it.

We walked together to the pub or hotel in the neighborhood, or town for a pint every now and then. The kitchen was generally left in a clean and useable state and we could sit in the lounge and watch TV together. I even invited colleagues and friends over.

One strange thing though, was that some of the guys did not like using the shower that regularly. Sometimes I would look on in shock as someone dashed out of the house, late for work, in clothes so crumpled they looked like he had slept in them.

Old Ms Monaghan would call over every now and then. She would glare at me, occasionally call me "you boy" and leave. The original diagnosis was correct. Old Ms Monaghan did not like me at all. So I took to avoiding her if I could help it. I ignored the door when I saw her ringing the bell from my bedroom window upstairs.

Unfortunately, trouble was not far from this new found paradise. The neighbours. They were a big family with lots of boys, two girls, I think, and a lot of fighting. There would be a lot of swearing between the husband and wife, sometimes between the children, other times between a parent and a child. The boys usually looked stoned. I avoided them. No one in the house said anything to them.

It did not help. Every now and then, I would park my car in the evening, and in the morning a new scratch will have been added to it overnight. Keyed, scratched, or kicked. One morning I found one side-view mirror had been kicked off. I knew who was behind it, the housemates guessed who might be doing it. It was not done to their cars and it had never occurred before. I could not do anything about it.

Things went further than that when I came home late one evening to find the patio glass partitions had been smashed.

This time, the following morning, I called the Garda. They came in acting all policey, CSI mini-me kind of. There were two police cars were parked outside. They took some pictures and looked around. Then they started questioning me. What was I doing in the country, where was I from, what I did, how long I had been staying there. They never asked any of or about my housemates. The only thing they did not ask me that day was what I had had for breakfast that morning. I felt like the criminal, the head of some kind of African mafia. At the end of it all they just gave me a reference number to give to the landlady for insurance purposes. How was I going to break the news to old Ms Monaghan?

The neighbours were watching all these shenanigans with particular interest, so much so that the queen mother came to the house later that evening to, of all things borrow a wine opener. She was really nice, made some small chit chat about the weather and left. The subject of the broken patio glasses never came up. She lived right next door, and walked through the patio that evening but never alluded to it even once. She brought the opener back and left. I never found out what she had concluded through her peace overture, but I had never spoken to that lady before the incident, and never spoke to her again.

Things calmed down after that, for a while.

Those housemates moved out, to be replaced by new ones. Of old Ms Monaghan's choosing this time, two Irish boys and a girl. Old Ms Monaghan did not take the risk of delegating the all important task of finding the correct tenants this time.

Then the slide to hell began all over again.

The kitchen started getting messier and messier. No matter how many times we talked about it, things simply got worse. The living room slowly became a no go area. Boxes of half eaten pizza

44

would be left everywhere, and the Big Brother channel was on TV non-stop. The "things" started staying afloat in the toilet for longer periods of time. I started to hibernate in my self-contained room. Inviting colleagues and friends over started to become embarrassing.

Then the appliances started breaking down. First up was the washing machine, followed by the stove, and then water spilled everywhere when the fridge went off, defrosted and never came back on again. They even managed to damage the shower. Fortunately for me, I had a separate bath in the self-contained room I occupied. The boys did not seem in the least bothered by this broken shower. It was a minor nuisance, only the girl whinged about it.

I learned a while later that, all along these chaps had been pinning all this damage on me. And of all people, this information came from old Ms Monaghan herself when she tried to teach me how to use the new washing machine. She brought in someone to replace the washing machine and decided to give me a lesson in how to operate it so "I couldn't break it again." They even blamed me for the broken shower in their bathroom for good measure. But I never used it! I reminded old Ms Monaghan that I had been in the house for a while now, and up until recently, all the gadgets had been working fine. How could I go on a rampage all of a sudden? She did not look convinced when she left.

These new housemates were vulgar, rude and hostile too. It was a throwback to the old nonsense. Walking into the living room one weekend, I found some racist literature strategically placed on the coffee table. I had never seen professionally published racist material before then. Where and how would you encounter such garbage? I burned it, promptly gave notice and moved out the following month, vowing never to share accommodation with the locals again.

Everyone was an investor in real estate or had bought strings of properties to let. So it had become relatively easier to find apartments.

45

I received a lot of literature and flyers trying to entice me to buy a house. We were smack in the middle of the bubble, so moving further away from locations that had town or city in the name yielded big discounts in price. It was one of the reasons why the so called commuter towns started to flourish. Though I shopped around extensively but could not find anything worth the asking price. I flirted with this idea for a while longer before finally deciding to give it a go, tentatively. I was going to 'test live', for a few months, in the lovely town of Ballymahon before committing myself. It had a picturesque river flowing through the centre of town and was only a few minutes' drive from my place of work. A lot of new housing estates were being built which qualified for the government subsidy. It looked like the perfect opportunity to gatecrash the property party.

I got an apartment through an estate agent and moved in. Things deteriorated right from the word go. The place had a small village mentality with a parochial mindset. I could not move about without being harangued.

The car park in my apartment complex was a popular spot for people to come and do drugs.

After returning from work in the evening, I would find a group of people crammed in a car in the car park, usually in their teens to early thirties, getting high. Sometimes they would quickly scramble off when they saw my car approach. Other times they would spill out of their cars and become quite abusive. On a number of occasions words were exchanged. Once in a while a person I did not know would be wandering around the complex and they might knock on my door, for no reason at all. Once, I had guests over when someone knocked on the door and just stood there. They did not believe that it was normal, in that place, for me at least. I took to avoiding my own place and spent as little time in the place as possible.

As if that was not enough, every now and then I would find an egg on my car's windscreen. Not as a present, but a smashed one. Four months into the lease, I dashed outside in a hurry to get to work because I was running late, only to find that my tires had been slashed.

I went and reported the matter to the police. They did not have a permanent station in that village. The police only came in for a few hours per day. Some days they did not even show up at all. A while later someone told me that there was an estate or apartments in the town used as a rehabilitation centre for some ex-convicts. Wow! Now you tell me!

The Gardai came and looked at the car, took some notes and proceeded to grill me about my immigration status, what I did, where I worked, who I lived with, my life story really. He even asked for the "non-identity card" Gardai card. Where had I seen this script before? I thought I had gone to report a crime! After completing the formalities, I went to buy some tires. I never heard from the Gardai.

When I put in my notice not to renew the lease, the estate agent withheld part of my rent. She cooked up a bunch of excuses about some bulb and marks on walls. She also refused to pass on the information I needed to claim a tax refund on the rentals. I tried everything but failed. I had no idea what to do, and she was an old dog at this game. I grudgingly moved on.

Buying a house in that town was out of question. It was just as well that I had lived in the place. It was quite surprising to find that an acquaintance had bought a property in that same town. A nice enough house but the location was a definite minus. I knew he could not sell it because the property market was in the toilet. He was in all probability in negative equity. He tried to rent it out. But that did not appear to have gone very well. I was even more surprised to see him in such good spirits when I visited him. What a tough or strange fellow he was.

The next port of call was Athlone. Conveniently situated close to where I worked. This time I went with a private landlord and took pictures of the place when I moved in. The landlady seemed like a nice, trustworthy lady, but I did not want to take any chances. It had become very easy to find places to stay now because the market was saturated. The catch was that landlords were becoming even more unscrupulous.

This place was full of old people. It was a kind of retirement compound. They appeared irritated when they saw me, but they pretty much left me alone. Some would greet me and strike a whole conversation about the weather. I had finally found sanctuary, in a geriatric ward!

When it was time to leave, I immediately found out how wrong I had been. And boy was I wrong about that lady! She waited until I was all packed and ready to go to the airport before sending someone to come and inspect the apartment. Her brother I think. He looked around the property and then returned only half my deposit, mumbling something about "Paying the final electricity bill and then depositing the balance in my account later." He even had the audacity to ask for my account details. I told him that I had settled the electricity bill already. He only looked at me blankly.

I could see the look of disgust on Charlie's face, a friend who was driving me to the airport. I knew straight away that something was amiss but had no time to tussle with him, so we drove off. It turned out that the brother was the actual owner of the apartment. After a few phone calls and text messages back and forth, it dawned on me that this lady had no intention of giving me back the balance on my deposit. She even refused to give me the details required to claim a tax refund I was entitled to. They were shafting the taxman too.

I took my case to the Private Residential Tenancies Board, an arbitration tribunal for disputes between tenants and landlords. I quickly realized how little I knew about my landlady and how well she had covered her tracks. The only details I had were her mobile number and bank account details. No address, not even her surname. The place where I had taken the deposit was apparently not where she worked. They confirmed this when I called on them. Were they in on the scam? The bank clerk smiled politely when I tried to ask for more details about the account I had been stashing money in for months. A brother and sister gang, this was certainly new territory.

Needless to say, she refused to give me any details to help with the case. I went to the deeds office and got the records about the owners of the property. It was her brother's. When I told her about the case that I had started with the board, she laughed at me, saying that as she was not the legal owner of the property, "I had no case." Without the physical address the board could not serve her.

Using the title deeds, her social website profile and the phonebook I managed to piece together her identity and pretty much most of her life story. I dug up her address, where she had been on holidays, the person she was in a relationship with, her favourite food and even her birthday. I passed the relevant details on to the Board. Houston, we have lift off!

She tried to give them the run around too. Eventually they managed to drag her kicking and screaming to the hearing. She ended up paying the deposit back with an additional token amount. She had wasted too much of their time. The money did not even come close to reimbursing all the costs I incurred when pursuing the case. I had tried my best to get my money back.

Jokingly (I hope), a work colleague in Galway asked me if Africans still lived in trees. In Ireland, I would really have preferred to live in a tree. It might have been slippery, uncomfortable, cold and wet, but maybe, just maybe, it would have been a lot less stressful.

Chapter 4

Let Us All Get Along

At the beginning of my stay I felt like a celebrity when walking around Galway. Not quite, I actually felt like some kind of novelty. Cars would slow to a crawl just so the driver could take a really good look at me. A few times, people would find excuses to try and touch my hair. Adults and kids, in a pub or on a plane. I would not have believed it myself if I had not been the object. It was a bit unsettling. This curiosity trailed me during most social interactions, especially in pubs. Conversations followed an invariably predictable pattern.

A greeting would be followed by the chart topping opening line of something about the weather, anything. Ranging from how nice the day was, how much it had rained yesterday, to what the weatherman is predicting for the next week. How this could be the coldest winter in ten years might be thrown in for good measure. I felt like an encyclopedia of useless information after such chit chat. Then the conversation would drift off into progressively more intrusive questions such as:

"What do you do for a living?"
"Where do you work?"
"Where do you live?"
"How old are you?"
"Where are you from?"
"What is the weather like?"
"What is your name?"
"Are you married?" (Yes, that would be the men.)

The only variation would be the order in which the questions were asked.

We would hover around the name part for a little bit longer to try and get the pronunciation right. Once that verbal speed bump had been negotiated, we would now be like old buddies. My inquisitor would then call a friend over and introduce us, allocating an entirely new country to me during the process. For some reason, Zimbabwe always came up tops. Mugabe was quite unpopular in Europe then and the disappointment would be obvious when I corrected them. An opportunity to grill one of Mugabe's kin had just been snatched away. The lull in our conversation would only be broken by the need to sort out which country I had earlier claimed to have come from, and where on the map it might be.

If they had a bit of information about my country then what they knew would come tumbling out. A relative might have worked or lived there, something about a former president or the capital city would be mentioned. This would reignite the conversation. Questions about whether the country was a dictatorship would follow. Was there a war raging? Statements about how corrupt African countries were and why there are so many of them (countries) would be made. This would be rounded off by how poor the wretched souls there were. "Did they really survive on less than one dollar a day?"

A number of relatively mature people would mention, with a chuckle, how priests used to urge them to "Donate money for the poor Black babies." This attitude must have carried over to the present times because most appeals for charity carried images of "poor Black babies".

Images of poor Black children, in dirty rags, would be on TV, in magazines, and newspapers. They would also be staring back at me from posters plastered around schools, churches and in the streets. Adverts with usually a sad sounding woman would be played on radio imploring all to give generously to the "poor Black babies". The imagery had changed, but the message was similar, donate to the "poor Black babies".

The question about how long I had been in the country always came up, usually followed by "How do you like it here?" This was the anchor question. How I responded was of the utmost importance. If I responded with "Oh it's fantastic, the people are so friendly. The place is so nice and green." And throw in the "apart from the cold" bit at the end. Such a reply would leave my newly discovered best friend beaming with approval. He would then give me a backhanded compliment about "how good my English was" and ask where I had learned it. He might even order a round of pints.

On the other hand, the music would stop if I said that I did not like it because there was nothing else to do but booze, moaned about having suffered a lot of racist abuse, and complained about how terrible the weather was. This response brought our conversation to a screeching halt, pouring ice cold water on our new found friendship. On some occasions the now former friend would call his real friends over and report to them, in disbelief, about how he had "found one who doesn't like it here." Another time I was strongly advised "to leave then." The atmosphere would be poisoned by this unwelcome indiscretion and we would drift as far away from each other as humanly possible within the confines of the pub.

My new buddies might also quiz me about how long I intended to stay in Ireland and if I intended to make it my permanent home.

In some places everyone would just ignore me, including the barman or shop attendant. That all important barman. I remember walking into a pub in Ballymahon when one patron sitting at the bar, smiling wryly to himself, asked the barman if he had "seen anything strange that day." I was not served in that place.

The barman or maid was the single most important thing in the pub, not the customer, not the beer, not even the owner of the place. When you entered the place, you needed to position yourself respectfully and quietly at the counter so the bar-person could see you, but ignore you. Do not speak until you are spoken to. They were very good with the first at the bar, first served. If they took an instant dislike to you, you may have to wait a bit longer. One barman would always hold a pint he was about to serve me beneath the counter before handing it to me. The drink smelled of urine on two occasions. I could not believe it, so I asked a friend to sniff it. I stopped going there. Sometimes matters heated up very much culminating in my leaving the place.

After a while the predictability made such overtures irritating. I could have been walking around with flash cards in my pocket and been able to survive whole evenings without uttering a single word.

A few times I was asked if I was a Nigerian and an asylum seeker. One sweet sounding and possibly well meaning lady told me about how she "saw very few coloured people about," and advised me to go to a certain church where I "would meet more of my kind."

Traditional Irish music was a big thing in pubs that I found charming. It was usually played by volunteers. Musicians would come and go during the course of the night coming with their instrument of choice, be it bodhran, a fiddle and others.

Interestingly, I never saw a harp being played. After a while the music sounded repetitive. It was the same fast paced repetitive beat with no accompanying vocals. The vocal music sometimes comprised touching lamentations or poems about the potato famine, the struggle against the English, or any such emotive subject and usually performed by a soloist with no accompanying musical instrument. There was a touch of irony in the differences between the traditional music and what is produced by world famous Irish bands or musicians.

Fooled by intrigue! Is that a South African pub? The name and décor are really a dead giveaway.

Pubs that had "trad" shows were usually crammed with people. Loud cheering and clapping would greet the end of each piece. There was no dancing.

Watching Irish standup comedians opened a small window into Irish humour. Jokes laced with swear words or which picked on minority or different groups would draw the loudest laughs. Jokes about Dubliners, the natives of Limerick, people from Cork, and other such local stereotypes sustained standup careers. That was before they got to the Nigerians, Chinese, and others. You needed to be local to get it.

A soon to be busy night at the office.

Festivals were a must have. Seemingly every other town had some kind of festival going. Galway had the film festival (Film Fleadh), The Galway Arts festival, the races, Kinvarra had the match making festival, Kilkenny had a comedy festival, even Tullamore had some kind of show going, and of course everybody had St. Patrick's Day.

I did not see many Black people attending these festivals. I saw some performers, but few attendees.

The drunken and rowdy crowds made my enjoying these events near impossible, especially during the evenings. I remember a group shouting at me "f**king n****r, Black b******d" in the street.

I was waiting to be served in one pub, when a number of gentlemen came up and stood behind. One stood directly behind me. Suddenly, the people in the pub roared with laughter. I looked around nervously not knowing what was happening. Then I looked up in the mirror behind the bar and realized that all along he had been making monkey gestures behind my head. The joke had literally gone over my head. He ran off when I turned round to confront him. The whole pub had found this prank extremely funny.

One evening I was unchaining my bike when, unprovoked, a group of young lads and girls walking on the opposite side of the street started shouting abuse at me. I had had enough! I started to walk across the street with the chain in my hand. They simply walked faster saying how "they had only been messing." I started to avoid such events.

Finding somewhere to sit in a pub or elsewhere for that matter was stepping into the unknown. The people next might shift uncomfortably or move to seats further away, away from this smelly and dirty thing which had deposited itself next to them. Others would start making derogatory or racist remarks. Such situations would have an added edge if there were women around. The overarching stereotype seemed to be that a Black man's dying wish was to sleep with that White woman. Yes, that White woman sitting right there. She could be a candidate for Miss Universe or an ugly plumb that would be able to show up for a Halloween party without a costume, it did not matter.

On a trip from London to Dublin, I went to my seat and found a couple already seated, with the girl having taken the middle seat. As soon as I got to my window seat, I saw them exchange a cursory and knowing glance. They stood up and swapped seats. It all happened without a single word being uttered.

Street performances were open to everyone.

Come one, come all, especially for the performers.

To avoid unnecessary awkwardness I resorted to looking for spots as far away from "them" as possible.

Visiting restaurants or hotels sometimes left me with a feeling of being in the wrong place at the wrong time and that my money was not paying their wages. Waiters would be quite condescending, the service shoddy and the food just not worth the trouble. The service, food and attitude improved over the years as did the mix of restaurants and staff.

A famous golfer who visited Ireland for a major golf tournament stayed at one of the most exclusive hotels in the country. A hotel maid met him in the corridors and asked him "what he was doing there." No Black person belonged there. What chance did a mere mortal like me stand? It was the same at airports. Check-in staff would be brash and rude. They would even react with shock when they realized that I was flying business class. It added to the stress of flying.

It was interesting to listen to the topics discussed on some national radio stations. There were a number of popular shock jocks who had fashioned themselves along the likes of Limbaugh or Beck in the US. One such popular show was on in the morning. People would tune to the station in stores and offices. A lot of people would call in and express their views on whatever hot topic was being discussed on the day.

I remember listening to one particular episode when a woman who had been in a relationship with a Black man called in to complain. When the woman finished her moaning, The Presenter did not address the relationship issues. Instead, he talked, or rather yelled about how certain types of immigrants –Africans - were lazy, abused the benefits system, and were not welcome in Ireland. He further asserted how only Chinese immigrants were better for Ireland and that they were welcome. After listening to a few of his shows I avoided it if I could.

You were allowed to contribute as much as possible into that benefits system. I never heard anyone complain about that.

When The Presenter died, he was lauded in the popular press. The Irish Examiner screamed that he had an "Instantly recognizable voice with rousing views." The national TV and radio broadcaster, RTE (an Irish version of the BBC), saw "Thousands of tributes and expressions of condolence flood into RTÉ." My experience in the few times I had listened to the man was completely at odds with what I read.

One writer had a tendency to express very strong views, to put it mildly, about immigrants and immigration in general in his columns in a popular broadsheet. I stopped buying and reading the newspaper The Writer wrote for. The bigoted views espoused in those columns became too much to stomach.

Ireland had a lot of churches. Catholic churches mostly. Fortunately or unfortunately, depending on which side of the aisle you were, the church's moral authority had been completely eroded. It was by now a spent force mostly due to a string of allegations and cases of child abuse. They were coming out thick and fast. They were shocking and very sad revelations. Those were some of the Christians.

I enjoyed cycling and would go out on my bike cycling around town. Cars would slow down next to me on the way and a head would pop out followed by a comment saying "How good my tan looked." The car would then speed off. Sometimes the remarks were flippant, other times they were much more barbed and racist.

Before going for work, I would get up around 05:00 A.M and cycle around town for about ten kilometers. A lot of trucks made their deliveries about this time. The roads were not what one would classify as cyclist friendly. Now picture this, I am briskly pedaling away when an eighteen wheeler pulls up behind me, slows down and follows me for quite a distance with the engine revving loud enough to scare me off the road and into the bushes or the wall. Most times there would be no vehicle in the other lane. The opportunity to overtake me safely would be available. This happened enough times to put paid to my little cycling hobby.

Socializing was a minefield littered with insurmountable obstacles. Sometimes I gave up. Other times I picked myself up, dusted myself off, and went out the following day – for more – it would seem.

Chapter 5

We Are What We Do

The flight was scheduled for later that evening. How I hated flying these days! I needed something to keep me distracted for the next six hours or so. I packed my bags. Something did not seem right. I unpacked everything, changed a couple of things and packed again. A quick glance at the watch, I had only managed to shave a whole of fifteen minutes. Fifteen minutes! What a disaster!

Five hours and forty five minutes to burn. I rummaged through the magazines in one of my drawers, found one that I had bought a couple of days earlier but never got round to reading it. I stretched out on the bed and immersed myself in the stories.

There was a story about the results of the referendum on the Lisbon Treaty. The EU had wanted a yes vote. The government had gone through a lukewarm and uninspiring campaign that had ended in the inevitable. The people had voted NO. There was a lot of back-slapping among the groups that had opposed it. They were very happy that they had given Europe the middle finger. However, this was considered to be the wrong answer, so the government called for a second vote. They must have explained the issues a shade more articulately the second time, because they voted yes! This exact scenario was repeated during the referendum to accept or reject the Nice Treaty. The message seemed to be that if the government did not like the answer, then you will keep voting until you get it right.

Another referendum was held during my time in Ireland. It had to do with the changing of a citizenship clause in the constitution – or a loophole that had allowed heavily pregnant Nigerians to come into the country and deliver a couple of weeks later to a bouncy Irish citizen. The mother would then be entitled to an Irish passport based on the child's parental rights with the possibility that the father would follow suit a couple of months later. This topic generated a lot of excitement and heat. This loophole was not meant for Nigerians or other Africans for that matter. It was one of the least controversial issues and went through without a fuss.

Why had I not opened this magazine before? I flicked the pages to a story about contaminated pork and other meat products. This provoked a huge outcry especially from the farmers as you might imagine. Pork was taken off the shelves locally and the export market dried up. That meant abattoirs shut, distribution outfits closed and lots of jobs lost. Farming was subsidized by the EU but there was no bailout or compensation forthcoming from the EU.

There had been a similar issue which had happened when dioxins were found in chicken. Havoc was wreaked each time foot and mouth disease flared up. It was interesting to see how the foot and mouth disease would rave and rage in the UK, jump into Northern Ireland and then just fizzle out when it reached the border with the Republic of Ireland. Never to be heard of in the Republic.

A story about an ongoing tribunal attracted my attention. Tribunals were almost a permanent fixture of the political scene at that time. There were a number of national inquiries simultaneously on the go. Mostly to do with corruption. There was one involving a very senior government official. Presentations about brown envelopes changing hands were made. The public was drip fed a constant stream of such strange tales such as how the very senior government official had no bank account at some point in his life. Other prominent personalities and the equivalent of Irish aristocracy were not spared.

The sports section had a feature on how Kilkenny had won the All Ireland for two or more years in a row. This was the hurling national championship. Hurling was a sport played with dangerous looking sticks called hurleys. They could have easily been used to whack off the opponents' arms but they used it to maneuver and hit a tiny ball called a sliotar around a field. It was similar to field hockey except that you could pick up the small ball and run with it and the gear was less cool. Hurling was a big deal, a national sport.

In fact hurling and Gaelic football were the two big ones. Gaelic football looked like a cross between football (local fans always insisted on calling that soccer) and rugby. The county rivalries for both these sports were intense. Later, word had it the leagues were beginning to unravel because the star players were skipping the country to look for work abroad. I heard that some Black people were trying their hand at the sport.

There was a short story about the deportation of a huge Roma family from Romania that had found an unclaimed space at a major roundabout in the M50 motorway and set up camp. Romania had just joined the EU and they too wanted to get into the fast lane to the good times. This fiasco provoked a massive outcry in the country and, like any bad reality show, went on for weeks. One Romanian person I knew was so embarrassed about the whole episode. He just wanted them to go back home. A few years later, their Northern counterparts took a more direct approach against Romanians and their homes. They simply attacked them and vandalised their homes. The Romanians did not hang around long enough to find out what they had in store for them next.

Another group that was the equivalent of an annoying national itch and refused to be scratched away was the Travellers. They only featured in the bad news segments of the media. I never heard a good word about Travellers. Apparently they were: "uncouth, bad mannered thieves who used to smash up hotels or pubs after a party. They had no respect for other people's property, space or even graves." Some hotels and pubs used to refuse them service. Ireland hosted an EU summit one time. The Travellers had inconveniently set up camp at a site by the side of the road from the airport. They could not have picked a worse place for a camping site and parking their caravans. It was right where other dignitaries would see filth and embarrass the nation. They settled on boarding up the side of the road to cover up the eyesore. For me, the caravan had been a symbol of leisure, freedom and holidays. Not anymore. It acquired a more deplorable and tacky twist.

I checked the time, over two hours gone! I put the magazine down. It was time to dash out for a quick bite from the corner shop.

As soon as I stepped out of the house, I ran into an old man out walking three dogs along the street. As I walked past going in the opposite direction, his dogs surrounded me and started baying at me viciously. Instead of calling them off, he just stood aside and watched. Fortunately, I was wearing some boots. I kicked one of the dogs. It yelped in pain. That was when he called them back and started telling me how two of them "would bite you". "This one will bite you." He kept repeating. I looked at him in disgust and walked away, unscathed, fortunately.

Upon reaching the shop, the lad at the counter seemed terribly hangover. He was hobbling around with bloodshot eyes and reeked of alcohol when he asked me what I needed. He should have been in bed. But how did he manage to work up such a giant hangover since the day before had been Good Friday! Not a drop of alcohol was meant to be sold on Good Friday and Christmas day. The exception being airport departure lounges, if you were lucky enough to be flying out on the day. And in pubs that opened to a select few, in secret, as rumour would have it. The simple solution people found was to stock up big time the day before. I saw trolley loads of alcohol the day before Easter. Why was Easter not like St. Patrick's Day? A day of goodwill, parades, and boozing, lots of boozing. There was so much boozing it should have been called St. Boozer's weekend.

How time flies, it was finally time to head for the airport. During the drive to the airport, I tuned in to a radio station that had a

64

heated debate about the plummeting fish stocks in the rivers. Angling was very popular in Ireland. You could always count on the Germans walking into Sean's Bar during the summer smelling of fish. Smelling of fresh fish and chatting nonchalantly to you about the day out on the river Shannon. It attracted anglers from everywhere. The depleting fish stocks were blamed in part on the East European immigrants by one caller. "They take it home and cook it" he said.

I made it in good time got through the formalities with little hustle and went to sit in the bar lounge, minding my own business. A man came up greeted me pleasantly and sat down. He had just collected his winnings from a bookmaker's that day. He had won big on the horses. Gambling was big. They bet on horse races, greyhounds, sports games and pretty much any event for which bookmakers could conjure odds for. It was rumoured that some people earned a livelihood this way.

He was very excited and in a generous mood. He even bought me a pint but then proceeded to share his dislike for Black people with me. It should have been confusing that he would sit next to me and even buy me a pint and profess to dislike me all in the same breath. After the experiences I had had, I came to a very disconcerting realisation that some of my tormenters actually reveled in "telling them (me)" how they felt, or goading me for some sort of reaction, or simply hurting me as any sadist would. What was his beef with Black people? "The men treat the women wrong." I told him that my Irish neighbours fought all the time. I had seen an Irish man walk into the Prince Bar with a woman covered in bruises and a black eye. He looked at me in disbelief and left.

Shortly, it was time to board. How time flies.

Chapter 6

An African Professional?

The resumes I had submitted during the job fair in Johannesburg secured me a number of interviews. I was particularly interested in one company. The products were widely used and the skills in high demand, therefore working for that particular company would be like a dream come true. During the interview, after getting the technical aspects out of the way, I enquired about life in Ireland in general. The lady on the other end of the line, Moira, told me about how nice and friendly the people were and how lovely the place was. She only complained that she thought the people smoked too much. Everything else was alright. She further told me that she had just returned from the United States herself and that she was apparently having a blast in Ireland!

The work in Galway was brilliant. I joined one of the most successful technology companies in the world. I interacted with people located in India, the States, Japan, Spain, South Korea, China, and lots of other different places on a regular basis. I even picked up a few words in some of those languages and bits of useful trivia along the way. I worked with smart people, mostly. The work could be stressful but fun.

A few days after reporting for work, I went out for drinks with some work colleagues who included Pat, his girlfriend and Mendez, a Spanish colleague who had joined the company literally on the same day I did. Shortly after we hit pubs, it dawned on me that Pat was eager to see me get really pissed. In between the pints of beer, he would order shots of hard spirits. It was a normal drinking tradition on a night out, as I found out, but this was way over the top. We were hopping from pub to pub, downing pints with interludes of shots of spirits, to lift the spirits or hasten the process.

Every so often Pat would literally inspect me to check how drunk I was. I thought this to be strange. As the night wore on he could not contain himself anymore and remarked, in a somewhat puzzled tone, about how I had not passed out by then. Pat kept boasting about how the Irish were the toughest alcohol drinkers in the world. This dubious claim to fame did not seem to help Pat with holding his liquor. He got dead drunk and started vomiting so much so that his girlfriend had to carry him. She actually half dragged him to the taxi.

In the early hours of the morning we decided to call it a night. On our way out to get taxis home, Pat did something completely unexpected. Out of the blue, whilst propped up by his girlfriend, he started shouting at me, "n****r, n****r, f**king n****r!" I was stunned. The whole evening, which had gone relatively well, came crushing down like a ton of rocks. Everyone in the group went quiet. I had to summon all my inner strength to restrain myself from punching him in the mouth. This had never happened to me before.

We showed up for work the following morning and everything seemed as normal as can be. It was as if nothing had happened. Pat even spoke to me about work. A few weeks later he decided to extend an invitation to me, again, for some drinks. I declined, and reminded him about what he had done the previous night out. He was apologetic and put his behaviour down to his visit to the United States! People usually blame alcohol. I told him that I was an African and I had been to the States before. Not a single person had called me racist names. I had also seen the rap videos and movies. We left it at that, the relationship was now frosty.

This same Pat became very offended at a later time when someone asked me what I had done over one long weekend. I replied that I had visited Londonderry. He came storming down from where he was and proceeded to lecture me about how it was not called that "down here." Apparently, when you are down in the Republic of Ireland you have to say Derry. It had something to do with England, colonialism or the sectarian troubles up North. No one would tell me definitively.

Cognitive dissonance was not hard to find. While watching a football match between Ireland and another country, a lad sitting next to me asked me who I was supporting, remarking with a smile that "I better be supporting Ireland." Then a few minutes later, he proceeded to shout racial epithets at a Black player in the Irish team. Right there next to me.

In addition to the national team, English clubs (and one Scottish club) had a massive following. Pubs would be packed during games. All the rivalries and merchandising had been imported very successfully. A lot of boys' parents' dreams were for their child to play in the Premier League.

This happened time and again. Most evenings when I went out with the local colleagues, someone would do something stupid. When I started avoiding these situations, the "anti-social" label was thrown around. I heard someone remark about "How surprised they were at how social I actually was" when I showed up every once in a while, having thrown caution to the wind.

Thursday was the preferred day for nights out. Mostly involving binge drinking. I wondered why nights out on Thursday of all days were so popular. Someone explained that weekly wages and benefits were paid on Thursday. Simple enough.

As such part of Thursday afternoon was dedicated to making phone calls or sending and replying to emails to make arrangements about what to do or where to meet up for the evening. After dinner, drinking would start in the nominated pub. It was each man for himself or a strict round robin when it came to buying drinks. The King's Head, Tir Na Nog, Blue Note, Naughton's, The Quays,

Murphy's, Monroe's, Roisin Dubh, The Cellar, you name them, there were plenty of pubs to pick from. At one time I thought there were more pubs than houses.

Just before midnight, people would drift to night clubs for dancing. Cuba, CP's, Karma, GPO, Warwick, among many. It seemed peculiar to me to see girls dancing on one side of the dance floor while boys danced by themselves on the other side. Couples (boys and girls that is) would only start dancing together later in the night, after the shots and pints had taken effect. The clubs would close around 01:00 A.M. Quite early, I thought.

After leaving the clubs, people would congregate around Supermac's (the Irish answer to McDonald's but lacking the pizzazz) or other fast-food joints. Fights over girls or nothing would erupt around these places. A Chinese person serving behind the counter or a Black person (me), waiting in line to be served seemed to have neon signs on top of our heads saying "Abuse me." We provided an even easier target for racist abuse.

Inevitably, scandal was never far away. Two workmates (I never heard of three) would be spotted kissing in a dark corner or sneaking off together. This provided fodder for Friday's office gossip and made the day go so much quicker. Invariably and stranger still, one or two people would call in sick on Friday morning. Some did not show up even on Monday. But I just had drinks with this guy yesterday I would wonder. "Why is an email being sent saying that this guy is off ill?"

This was new territory for me, but it was quite common. In due course this behaviour even became acceptable. It was not remarkable anymore when someone did not show up for work the day after one of the mothers of all booze ups. When I brought this up I was told, with a chuckle, about how "laid back" Ireland was. I thought it was just plain old fashioned laziness.

American colleagues always liked to visit Ireland for work. It was, in all reality according to them, "a holiday". They could only dream about the number of public holidays we had. In all the countries the company operated in, Ireland had the most Public holidays and statutory employee vacation.

We also went to the head office in the States for training. Even when we were away, my colleagues brought strange attitudes with them. In the end I avoided them.

Common courtesy or respect was hard to find among colleagues. People would be extra rude or outright abusive. The consequences were twice as severe if I retaliated. They never treated each other in a similar manner.

I only once made an official complaint concerning two particularly uncouth, obnoxious and abusive colleagues. The abuse stopped, but word went round about a certain someone needing to develop a thicker skin, race cards, PC police and other such terms. The next time someone called me a monkey I fumed, seethed with rage and gritted my teeth - silently. They would gang up on me again, I thought. I started wondering if my experience was unique to me. When I mentioned this to an Asian colleague, the only thing he had to say was that "The Irish, they are the worst!"

Dr. Bekoma, a medical doctor friend told me about an incident that happened to her in the hospital. She was on call in A & E at night when a patient was brought in who needed to be attended to immediately. The patient became aggressive and hurled racist abuse at her when she tried to attend to him. He did not want to be treated by a Black doctor. Other staff and nurses were present. She thought that I was a shade more fortunate because she dealt with the general public all the time. She seemed disturbed by this ordeal. I wondered out loud what I would have done in the same situation.

When applying for jobs, every time I presented my degree in engineering and other qualifications that I had earned in Africa, I could see the interviewers' noses going up in disbelief. Engineering, in Africa! I enrolled for a master's program in engineering at one of the Irish universities. Over a pint, I later learned from some work colleagues that the expectation had been that I would not make it past the second semester. Either my brains would be fried, in which case I would drop out or the exams would take care of me if I clung on. Word went round when I sent in my transcripts to justify my study followed by some sort of shockwave. I had passed and they were shocked. You could not hide anything even if you tried. They had reacted in a similar manner when I attempted a certification exam. Most people in the company had failed it. First with winks and nudges predicting my failure, then with shock after I passed. This constant questioning and need for justification and validation was annoying.

What people thought about me taking an advanced degree was, however, the least of my worries. The cost was. I was turned upside down and given a thorough and vigorous shake down until the last penny had dropped out of my pocket. It was daylight robbery!

The cost of living in Ireland was very high. Education was prohibitively expensive for the immigrant. And it went up every single year. Whereas I was coughing up most of my annual salary to pay my fees, my Irish classmates paid nothing. They even ignored a token fee of a couple of hundred euro that they were meant to pay.

So you can imagine my incredulity when one day, out of the blue a classmate, Padraig, started telling me about "How easy life was for immigrants, and how much of a soft touch Ireland was. And that all immigrants were freeloading on everything. Benefits, housing, education, you name it!"

Firstly, I reminded him about how much tax I had to pay to subsidise his and others' education and benefit claims. Then we talked about the amount of money I was forking out for the privilege of studying alongside him. Suddenly, it did not look so clear cut anymore. Other classmates who had earlier been supportive of Padraig's position were now not very sure about their assumptions.

It was unimaginable that budding intellectuals exhibited such ignorance. These guys could read and write, and possessed the research skills and tools to educate themselves. What hope was there for the uneducated?

When handing in my assignment sheet for one course I saw the lecturer put a mark on it. This little gesture was unremarkable enough, but I had seen Padraig's paper before mine being thrown on the pile without any mark being put on it. I pricked my ears. The answer scripts were pretty anonymous. Only student identity numbers were written on them. I stood by the door and watched the lecturer as everyone else submitted their assignment scripts. Two Irish colleagues submitted their scripts. Nothing happened, no scribbling. They went straight onto the pile. An Asian colleague handed his in. A small dash scribbled and the paper casually thrown on the pile. The telltale mark was appended to another Asian's and a Black students' script. I was shocked. Was he doing what I thought he was?

A friend had once told me about a time when her son had gone home very upset. The reason being they had been asked to explain the difference between a bucket and a Black person by their teacher. Supposedly the correct answer was meant to be: "The sh&t in the bucket." I digress.

A Nigerian classmate, Jones, had thought this particular course to be his forte. After the test, he was irritating everyone within earshot by thumping his chest, and bragging about how he was expecting an A grade. I tried to tell him about my little Sherlock Holmes investigation and suspicions. He dismissed them out of hand. When the results were released, he was near tears. Not tears of joy. I had tried to warn him. I do not think he even remembered or cared.

In passing, I mentioned my suspicions to a friend who was studying medicine at a different university. She laughed. It was a well known fact in her university about how impossible it was for non-Irish students to get very good grades or first class awards. She said that it had been so bad that one group of students complained to the university. No matter how hard they worked, or how intelligent they were, only Irish students would get top class grades. This particular group told them that they would inform their government about this anomaly so that future students would never be sent there. Of course they strenuously denied everything. I still wonder what impact the threat of losing the cold hard cash had.

A Nigerian I worked with, Abasi, once claimed that he had never experienced racism in Ireland. This was an astounding claim. His was a survivor. Abasi had worked in a pub as a cleaner whilst studying in college. I regularly sat in that pub, certainly not to celebrate. The racial class hierarchy prevalent in most work places was even more evident here. It was most visible in pubs, restaurants, hotels and night clubs. How blind must Abasi be?!

The African people would clean the toilets, dishes and mop floors. They would also man the night club toilets. The toilet-man usually had a collection of cheap perfumes laid out on a table close to the door. He would keep a close eye on the toilet in general, cleaning up after some drunk had vomited whatever sick inducing mixture had been imbibed. The toilet-man would mop it up and hand perfumes to the patrons on their way out. Some would tip him. Others would abuse him. I knew a Nigerian man whose wife was in charge of the ladies' toilet while he was in charge of the gent's. Rumour had it that other less legally acceptable substances were taken or peddled in the toilets.

The other jobs I saw being performed by Africans was that of caring for the old or disabled. This involved looking after Irish people who could not look after themselves. They included very old people who could not bath, dress, cook, clean or even take themselves to the toilet. People with Down's syndrome and mental illness were also looked after. I met a few African people who did this job. They went round the big cities cleaning up, helping, and taking care of the old. Irish people would not do these jobs.

Such mundane, dirty or low wage jobs were known as the *jobs that the Irish would not do*. During the boom years when I travelled on one budget airline, the air hostesses would predominantly be East European. The pay was beneath the Irish. The desks at Dublin airport were manned by the Irish.

One layer above these jobs you would find the waiters and waitresses. This is where you would find the East Europeans, a lot of them Polish. A few Irish people did these jobs. Then of course it would be further up to the bar tenders, mostly Irish with some East Europeans. The bar managers and supervisors were invariably Irish.

Abasi did one of those jobs which the Irish would not do.

He had two other Nigerian colleagues working alongside him. And here he was claiming that he had never experienced racist abuse in Ireland, I was astounded.

Abasi and I had crossed paths a few years earlier. I had met him at the US embassy in Dublin. I was there applying for a US visa. The headquarters of the company I was working for then was in the US. He was also applying for a visa. The waiting room was always crowded. So we got talking. His application was rejected. The consul lectured him in front of the crowd of other applicants. It was humiliating. I on the other hand, after some stern questioning, equally humiliating was granted the visa.

I thought I had seen the last of him, but that same day when I boarded the train to Galway, there he was again, looking very disappointed. He wanted to leave Ireland. But those plans were scuppered by that illusive visa to the other heaven. I sympathized with him and shared a drink. The combination of drink and a sympathetic ear was enough for Abasi to pour his heart out. In summing up his adventures, one interesting statement Abasi made that day was that "Normally there is one Judas in every twelve, but in his experience with the Irish it was the opposite." He got off the train in Athlone. I thought I would never see him again. I was wrong again.

I got off the bus at Limerick bus station and there was Abasi again, in all his glory, complete with a bandana and of all things, an American flag! Here is a guy whose visa application had been so humiliatingly rejected by that American woman and he was wearing the US flag on his head. I could not get what was going on in that head. He was on his way to Cork. He asked me why I had come back from the States. We had a brief chat and went our separate ways.

Abasi was not going away. I was very surprised when our paths crossed again, in Athlone this time. By this time, he had decided to go about the acquisition of an Irish passport the old fashioned way. He found himself an Irish girl, had a child with her, and applied for a passport as a parent of an Irish citizen. They settled down and bought a house together. Then she dumped him and kicked him out of the house.

Ogli, Abasi and I were knocking some balls around in a pub when some Irish gentlemen challenged us to a game. White versus Black, what a game! It was a silly but tense game. We beat them. Abasi got overexcited. He was smiling from ear to ear and started saying how the "n*$$as had won." I was incensed and told Abasi in no uncertain terms about what I thought. Ogli was there but did not intervene.

Ogli was an easy going optimist. I only saw him jolted out of his easygoing stride once, when unprovoked, a child of about twelve called him "n****r" on the street. He asked the boy who had taught him such things. He did not hang around long enough to elaborate.

Abasi said I did not have respect for him. I thought the question should have been whether he had any respect for himself. Was it desperation or did he lack any semblance of pride all?

I realized much later, way too late, that I had been asking the wrong question all along.

Life was tough for seasoned professionals, people with fully baked skills, ready and willing to contribute, to accomplish good things, great things even. Life was tough for dedicated, hardworking and honest people. Only now can I open my eyes and try to imagine what it must have been like at the bottom. Folks full of dreams, hopes and expectations, only starting out in their careers, in life.

It was really tough at the bottom, but it must have been really, really tough right down there at the bottom.

Ogli, a consummate professional and an optimist's optimist found work somewhere else and left Ireland.

When worked abroad, they were expats, we were just economic migrants. I did not even need to show up to be despised. I felt that no matter how hard I worked, my achievements would never be acknowledged. I would never be respected as a professional or a human being. That is not what I signed up for.

By now it had gradually dawned on me that I had been fooled. Not deliberately. I had naively conflated Moira's world with mine, forgetting that our differences meant that we inhabited completely different and extreme sections of the local friendliness spectrum.

Chapter 7

Dog Eating Dog

Having knocked off from work on a particularly tough day, I decided to go and relax over a pint before heading home. I was surprised to see a Black gentleman sitting alone by the counter, sipping a beer, as I walked into Kelehan's pub. How refreshing I thought as I eagerly sauntered over and warmly greeted him.

His response: "I am a doctor."

So I told him that I on the other hand was an engineer. He looked at me suspiciously.

Is that the way they greet each other in his country? Using their professions or occupations? How strange, I thought to myself. The gentleman was from a neighbouring country. The conversation did not go anywhere. So I beat a hasty retreat to the inner sanctuary of the pub and sat down, alone. To continue brooding on prior events of the day and this new addition. What happened there? It was safe to go to bed once the memories had been sufficiently suppressed, very far back into the subconscious by each subsequent pint.

The gentleman had no obligation to warm up to me simply because we shared a skin colour.

There is an African saying that could roughly translate as: "Beggars never like each other." It would sum up some interactions amongst us, the guests in the land. The local environment had been made so toxic by stereotypes perpetuated locally that we bought into them and viewed each other with the utmost suspicion.

Every Black person was presumed to be an asylum seeker, until they explained themselves.

These negative perceptions permeated the way Black people viewed themselves and filtered into the interactions with each other. We now believed how we had come to be defined. This was in addition to the baggage we had brought with us.

Some Africans from more prosperous countries might have thought of themselves as being a class above the rest, but still accepted and tolerated being regarded as inferior to the Irish. For still others, it was all about self preservation. So they went around joining the locals in perpetuating nasty tales about other Black people in the hope that that would earn them a few crumbs of something, anything, from the high table. Others were dignified, confused, but dignified and generally seasoned professionals, but as a result too clever by half at times.

Still more had swallowed the myth that their governance system was superior in Africa even though their country folk back home were slaughtering each other every election time.

A few had bought into the story (again liberally fed to them) that, of all things, their accents and English was the best on the African continent.

Some West Africans always talked about `papers' and everyone knew or had heard of a crook or two from that part of Africa.

An Africa American I meet in Dublin feels Africans are "traitors" and that Georgia is not south enough, I need to go to the Deep South. We just look at each other next time we meet.

Zambians, South Africans, Congolese, Kenyans, Zimbabweans, Sudanese, Ghanaians, Togolese, Tswanas, Egyptians, Algerians, the list went on. And so did the stereotypes. And that was before you added the East Europeans, further divided into Polish, Lithuanians and so on. Throw in the Chinese, the Indians, the Brazilians, and you would start to wonder how they maintained that list of stereotypes. Someone had to.

It was petty but cruel. It was still allowed to separate us from our brothers and sisters. It was sad.

Locally, the Dubliners were thieves, the people from Galway clannish, folks from Limerick had an unhealthy fascination with knives, and you could not understand a word when someone from Cork spoke. A Dublin taxi driver once told me about how "The country people did not open their mouths when speaking, which was why it was difficult to understand them." It was not me, it was them. He was reassuring me about my accent. Theirs was innocuous enough. Our buying into the whole stereotypes thing was madness. And sad.

It always puzzled me when I saw a Black person proudly walking around in a green t-shirt with the word "Ireland" emblazoned across the front and the image of a shamrock. Once in a blue moon, a Black face would also pop up on TV and talk about how friendly and nice they found the local people and generally sung a lot of praises about how well they had been treated. I really wanted to find that corner of Ireland these folks inhabited as I had only caught a small glimpse of it in my day to day life and the rest existed in books and on websites promoting tourism to Ireland.

For some reason, I did not observe Polish (I saw them in red and white) or other non-African immigrants strutting around in green outfits nor did I see them on TV touting the virtues of the local hospitality. If anything, the contrast in attitudes could not be starker.

I once watched a debate about immigration on a UK TV channel. The panel consisted of three White men, one mixed race man and a Black woman. They were discussing a particularly thorny case involving the possible deportation of an African man. The Black lady was defending the UK's right to kick the immigrant out of the country while the three White and mixed race men defended the African man's right to stay in the country. It was surreal.

Chapter 8

Being Strong as an Ox

Shortly before lunch one day, I had a sharp pain in my abdomen. I tried to ignore it but it persisted. I was not sure whether it was because of what I had eaten the previous night. It was impossible to stay put at my desk. There was a doctor's surgery that I had noticed on the way to work. It was not far, so I made my way over there. This was my first time to visit a doctor's surgery in Ireland.

When the receptionist took down my details, she seemed particularly interested in how I was going to pay. I told her that I would pay by cash. After a brief wait she showed me into the treatment room. A few minutes' later a doctor came in. The first question he asked me was how I was going to pay. Again I said by cash. At this point I was getting quite exasperated. He did not believe me and asked me outright if I was an asylum seeker. I told him that I was not and showed him my work identity card and bank card. This seemed to convince him. He examined me and gave me a prescription. I paid in cash and left.

Visiting hospitals has always been an awkward experience for me. This visit breezed to the top of the charts in awkwardness. It was also upsetting. When I left his surgery I could not help but wonder what it was that he had prescribed for me. I bought the medicine. But that experience would still not leave me. I did not take the medicine.

Later, I wrote a complaint letter to him and a Health Board. He wrote a non-apology apology back to me copying the Health Board. Someone from the Health Board also responded. They told me to p*$s off (not their exact words). After that episode, I tried to avoid hospitals as much as I could. If I felt really bad, I would just buy a pain killer, some lemons and ginger and let whatever it was that was bothering me to wear itself out before it did me.

One tooth started to bother me. After a week or so of playing the hard man I succumbed to the pain and made an appointment with a local dentist. When I arrived, there was a Nigerian woman clearly in a lot of pain having a tussle with the dentist who had refused to treat her. It turned out there were issues with getting payment from people seeking asylum.

I was asked about how I was going to pay when my turn came. Because of my ability to pay I was pretty much frightened into scheduling another appointment for even more expensive treatments. She wanted to remove all my wisdom teeth. A bit of wisdom returned after the anesthesia cleared, I cancelled the appointment.

When I moved to Athlone, I had to undergo a medical check-up as part of the preliminary formalities for work. I went to the company designated medical practice expecting an x-ray, some health related questions, a stethoscope to my chest, a urine test and possibly some blood being requested. No, not this doctor, he never asked for any of those. He asked me to undress instead. I just stood there in shock. He repeated it. It was almost like he drew some sort of satisfaction from looking at my genitals. He asked me a few health related questions and signed the forms. I dressed and left. This was the strangest medical exam I had ever had in my life.

Next time I was ill I resisted. Whatever I had was not clearing so I went to see the company doctor again. Memories of my previous experience had not receded. I reassured myself that, this was just a cough. To my horror he asked to me to undress again. I never went back to that practice.

Next time I fell ill was on a trip from Dublin. For some reason I could not stop vomiting all the way through the trip. To make matters worse I was driving and alone. So I reluctantly decided to check myself into the nearest A & E. It was in Navan. I was surprised to find a Black doctor there, even a Black radiographer. I wondered if I was dreaming. They did a battery of tests on me. When the time for the results came an Irish doctor called me. I refused and insisted that I see the doctor who had seen me before. She was dumbfounded. This was irrational. What had happened to me?

Chapter 9

The Tiger Has Left the Building

Moods bloomed during the boom
All over the moon with the boost
Come noon, it was all gloom
As doom loomed

Wailing sirens calling for a national panic heralded the onset of the recession. They did not, but every person looked up from whatever they were doing when the R-word reared its ugly head. Even the dogs, cats and horses smelled it. Yesterday adores masters started to throw them out, in droves, literally. Organisations that care for animals started to receive or find even more abandoned pets. It touched (and torched) every aspect of Irish life.

First it was pay freezes, followed by pay cuts and then the inevitable, a frenzy of mass firings or redundancies. Factories, hotels, restaurants, shops and government departments were shutting down. People were losing jobs left right and centre. You could now hear a penny drop on the far end of a shopping mall. They were drained of shoppers. This was followed by shutters on the shop fronts coming down permanently as they went burst.

The government's decentralization project that had so preoccupied national discourse only a few months earlier, was consigned to the garbage bin. After a "consultation process", the lengthy and expensive migration of public sector jobs to different parts of the country faltered. No new jobs would be made to magically appear that way. The line for benefits, the dole, was growing. The government was broke. The property market, the goose that laid the golden eggs went from life support to the mortuary in a flash. It did not rest in peace however, because the bad smell of mortgages in negative equity, underwater properties, abandoned and crumbling housing estates started growing. It was now becoming putrid.

There was hysteria on radio, on TV, in pubs and on the streets accompanied by a lot of yelling and pointing of fingers. There was a new show in town. The recession had arrived. Had the boom been an elusive mirage? No one was willing to admit that it had been good while it lasted.

In trying to figure out what had hit them, everyone suddenly became an economist, or some sort of expert. They all knew who to blame: Fianna Fáil, Bertie, Cowen, property developers, bankers, everyone else but themselves. As in most moments of crisis, people wanted to grab the government by the throat and squeeze it, hard. But alas, they were only allowed to vote them out. Every other day announcements about companies laying off hundreds or thousands of employees were made.

Dell, a national treasure, shut down most operations in Limerick, relocating thousands of jobs off shore. Bank of Ireland to lay off over a thousand. Atlantic Homecare closed a number shops, HP shut down some sites. Some multinationals were simply shifting operations to East Europe or Asia. Poland and India were mentioned a lot of times. And so it went on. No sector was left unscathed. Hiring in the public sector, a major provider of cushy for-life jobs, was frozen. Only retiring, resignations and firings were allowed. The exit door was wide open, but the entrance was firmly shut.

Say a prayer for the new graduates because job prospects had all but evaporated. New college entrants now faced the unwelcome reality of having to fork out some euro for their education. The time of plenty and freebies had truly come to an end. The cockiness, overconfidence, smugness and optimism had been replaced by pessimism, despondency and despair. The swagger was swallowed up by fear and a haunted, hunted demeanor. Thousands of young Irish men and women packed their bags and booked one way tickets to Britain and Australia, among many destinations. Déjà vu?

Then someone mentioned the IMF. Everybody went ballistic. Part of the hidden sentiment being that the IMF was meant for third world countries. Maybe they just knew full well how brutal an economic surgeon this organization was. Arms with a begging bowl were stretched towards the ECB for a bail out. New clichés entered the everyday national lexicon: bail-out, cuts, ghost estates, contraction, bubble, shock, double-dip, negative equity and more. Growth (or the lack of it) was no longer associated with plants or animals. Deepening had a lot to do with a hole, but not just the physical one.

Cowen, the new Prime Minister did not stay in the Taoiseach's residence long enough to even change the curtains. The peasants were at the gates baying for his government's blood. He could not afford bread and no circus would perform for him on credit. Bertie, whose shares had plummeted on the political stock exchange and had handed the chalice to the hapless and complicity Cowen, and other previous bigwigs were now nowhere near the carnage. Cowen reluctantly set the execution date for his government. A new government was elected within weeks.

The annual budget paradigm went out the window. The budget was revised every few months. Rolling government budgets became the norm. I had never seen anything like it before. Times became so desperate that when the real IMF waltzed into Dublin, people had already resigned themselves to an uncertain fate. There was not so much as a whimper to be heard.

A referendum was held to decide whether to accept the EU Fiscal Treaty or not. This included some savage cuts. It passed. Turkeys voting for Christmas! Who would have imagined it? The alternative, it was said, was all the turkeys starving themselves to death, economic suicide.

There was mayhem in construction. Builders could not shift their stock. Ghost estates sprung up where shiny new houses had stood. Banks sat on a pile of bad debts. In an effort to offload the properties, prices were cut and Dutch auctions held. Repossessions became rampant as people fired from their jobs could not keep up the mortgage payments. House prices fell by as much as 53%.

A three bed semi-detached house I went to see in Edgeworthstown had been on the market for two hundred thousand euro (€200,000). The reservation fee was three thousand euro. For an additional forty to eighty five thousand euro, they would provide and install all kitchen appliances, carpets or tiles, blinds and curtains, and lounge and kitchen furniture. Something about the shower door bothered me. Other than that, I had six days to commit. Years later, the same property was back on the market for ninety nine thousand euro (€99,000), all options included.

Immigrants and locals started jumping ship. Leaving through the ultra modern Dublin Airport, more impressive after the Celtic Tiger had weaved its magic. Houses were simply left vacant and cars abandoned at the airport. This further depressed the rental market, putting more pressure on the buy to let investors, speculators and builders. Bricklayers, plumbers, landscapers, architects, electricians, and builders sat around twirling their thumbs.

In 2001, Ireland was number eleven on the Global Competitive Index which gives countries the right to boast about how better they are. Those national bragging shares dropped to number twenty-five in 2009.

The banks were bailed out but credit terms were tightened.

This despair spawned a cottage industry in newspaper and magazine columns, and TV and radio talk shows dishing out advice (or cow dung depending on one's perspective) ad nauseam. They

86

covered matters ranging from finances, what to do, how to tell the kids, to filing for bankruptcy. Where were they when such services were needed most? Other pieces of cow dung included how to cope with depression and imploring people to "Start thinking outside the box."

People stood in tears outside factories as they received the bad news. As a mark of the much touted entrepreneurial spirit, someone with a morbid sense of humour suggested selling ropes near the factories that had just been closed, followed by opening an undertaker business.

People did start thinking outside the box alright. Crime levels went up, peaking around 2008/09. Burglaries, robberies, thefts, fraud, kidnappings, shop lifting you name it. One relatively common crime ironically called Tiger kidnappings involved holding a bank or post office employee's family while the said employee facilitated the theft of usually large amounts of cash. The hostages were released when the criminals made their getaway. Had someone held the country hostage?

I was halfway through my dinner when a Traveler gentleman came and sat next to me. He ordered a beer and bragged about how, though he was not buying food anymore, he was well fed. To prove his point, he took off his coat and took out some smoked salmon, bread rolls, cheese and a salad. The disappearing rabbit trick would have been put to shame. He made a salmon sandwich right there in front of me and ate it. He told me that he simply walked into Dunne's or a Spar and picked what he needed. He was a shoplifter.

As is usually the case when the economy hits the fan, *it* lands everywhere. Most would prefer *it* to only hit the immigrant. In Ireland, the immigrant started to bear the brunt of local frustrations. All these problems were due to the influx of Jo Foreigner, the reasoning went. They wanted the illusion to persist. So the mob was angrily hunting for any scapegoat deemed responsible for this outrage. How dare they expose the emperor's new wealth as fictitious!

Immigration rules were tightened even further. Every now and then a new rule change would be announced to close this or that loophole. The conventional wisdom was that as long as Jo Foreigner was flushed out or kept out of the country, all new job openings would be filled by locals. But, as is normally the case with rushed fixes to complex problems, they proved to be half baked.

Some inspiration at last, a shop owner demonstrates how to think outside the box.

Multinational companies requiring certain skill sets advertised for jobs and waited. Remember that Ireland was now playing in the big leagues, it was an advanced economy. They waited and waited for competent Irish candidates. The companies complained, threatening to relocate. Somehow the "This many job vacancies equals that number of Irish people off the benefits queue" logic was not working as anticipated. It was back to the drawing board again, to tinker with the rules.

When on a Budget Airline flight again, for the first time I saw an all Irish team of air hostesses. What happened to the East Europeans? Serving staff in pubs had changed too. What happened to the jobs that the Irish would not do?

Immigrants were being blamed for not only taking jobs from locals but also for taking all the benefits. Everything wrong in the economy would be resolved if only all the foreigners were kicked out. If the environment had been bad during the boom times, it was now suffocating. Foreigners were caught between the hard rock of hostile and chaotic officialdom and the hard place of inhospitable locals.

I was viewed with suspicion when I went about my business. People I did not know would walk up to me and start talking about how my kind, the immigrants, was depressing wages for the local workforce. They would ask questions like "Are you legal?" "When was I going back home?"

On the streets, people stopped, looked at me contemptuously, then spat or uttered racial epithets. My property was vandalized. Water and eggs had been thrown at me and I had been shot at with an air gun (fortunately?) on the streets, in broad daylight! The intensity and frequency was increasing.

Another African acquaintance's car was stolen and burnt. At another time he was set upon by some racist thugs on a bus (he had to use the bus now) from Dublin city centre to Blanchardstown and assaulted. Nigerian taxi drivers spoke of being attacked and racially abused when ferrying people around. A Polish man was brutally murdered right outside his workplace.

I stopped wandering around especially in the evening, and started spending more time looking over my shoulder than where I was going. The silence from the powers that be was deafening. I even contemplated arming myself.

Multinationals were leaving the country or scaling back local operations. Workers had become mobile, skilled and unskilled. The Tiger came, it looked, did its thing and left. Was it time to check out the departure lounge of the ultra-modern Dublin Airport?

Chapter 10

Facing Up to Goliath

Fortunately, even during the recession my field had fantastic job prospects. Some companies were complaining about how difficult it was to find the right candidates for some positions. Nevertheless, looking for jobs was still quite the adventure. From the application down to the interview stage and beyond, it was a convoluted process fraught with slippery steps on a winding staircase. Every now and then, I would tumble down. From my perspective, it was still an interesting process in its own right, in spite of the many pitfalls.

A former interviewer once told me that the first name and Irish qualification had confused them. They were expecting an Irish man, they were surprised to see a Black man walk into the interview room. I had seen that reaction on the faces of some panelists before and had been taken aback by it. It all made sense now. I was "blessed" with that Irish first name. The qualification from an Irish university widened the crack in the door. The combination of first name and Irish qualification sometimes helped secure my foot on the first step, the crucial shortlist for interviews. I heard of people who in desperation had resorted to changing their names by deed poll. From say, Nwikwe Olinukwu to something more locally palatable like Charlie O'Hagan. Apparently, this tactic changed lives. Of course some might have done it for other reasons, some of them underhand.

Then it was on to the interview. Once in a while I would impress, other times I would fall flat on my face, failing to convince them that I was that suitable candidate. Other times I would come out baffled as to what had happened. After making it past these first hurdles, the conditions of work and salary would loom even larger, the next and much more formidable mountain to climb.

I went through this process with a number of companies and did not make it for some. The offers from some were far below my expectations, so I turned them down. When it came to the salary with one multinational company, I thought it to be too low. I compared the salary information I had gathered from adverts (among other sources), they came up short. Their HR person, a smooth taking car salesman of a person, reassured me that it was commensurate with the rate they paid for that range of responsibilities, qualifications and experience. Going against all my instincts and better judgment, I joined the company.

The start was good. The work was very much in my field and challenging. Most colleagues were helpful. I was brimming with enthusiasm. We were operating at the cutting edge of technology in addition to the opportunities to learn and acquire more skills. I could also travel.

Slowly but surely, my eyes started to open to the reality of what was going on. First I was mostly used as a cat's paw. Perhaps naively, I had expected to work my way up. I did work my way up alright, but it was just with added responsibilities. It appeared there was an invisible line drawn in the sand when it came to remuneration. It was like feeding a turkey really well in readiness for Christmas. I came last, irrespective of the level of responsibility and competence.

During a general conversation with one of my managers, she told me that "Even the Irish had been discriminated against in the States and Britain. It was now their turn to do it."

Every appraisal was usually accompanied by my manager – a sincere and earnest sounding fellow - telling me how (apparently in confidence because he told me not to tell anyone else) I had received the highest pay rise in the section.

A small voice kept telling me to be careful about what secrets I kept, as they may not necessarily be working in my favour.

One evening after work, I was knocking some balls around with some Irish colleagues when the conversation turned to the recent salary increments. It gradually drifted into actual salaries. It was embarrassing and surprising to learn the gap between my salary and theirs.

When I asked my manager, the sincere and earnest sounding fellow, about my pay status in the section, he told me that as a matter of fact, I was the lowest paid. He however promised to talk to his boss about it to see what could be done. I had three degrees, had completed all sorts of certifications, had extensive industry experience, and was competent in my role (as evidenced by the results of their own performance management model). But I was still paid far less than even people I supervised.

Others performing similar duties obviously had better conditions, and that was before looking at the money. It was unbelievable. What other factors differentiated us and would warrant such inequity? I had heard the term "We look after our own" whispered around.

They clearly did not see it that way. After consulting with his boss, a much more unsavoury character, my manager sincerely and earnestly came and told me to go and jump in a lake.

I thought resigning was the better option.

When I went to hand in my resignation letter, the girl in human resources appeared surprised. She asked me what I was going to do afterwards. When I said I was going back to Africa, she looked at me as if I had gone mad asking what I was going to do out there. As a parting shot, they did not pay me my last month's salary.

I contacted a migrant assistance organization for help or advice but never got a response from them. I took my case to a Tribunal, at first representing myself. They came to the hearing with an expensive lawyer who ran legal circles around me. So I decided to lawyer up too, albeit at a much cheaper rate than them.

Having read so many stories about immigrant workers who had been discriminated against, swindled out of their wages, or underpaid, I was still taken by surprise to be a victim. I had believed that this happened mostly to people in low skilled jobs such as bricklayers or deckhands on ships. I found myself in unfamiliar but similar territory.

They of course denied everything and used all sorts of tactics to rubbish my case. They talked about how I had been un-contactable and ran away with passwords. Fortunately there had been emails going back and forth between myself and them. I had no administrator rights to their systems (a system administrator is like a god, I most definitely was not). They tried everything. It was awful.

As if that was not enough, my visa was about to run out so that clock was also ticking down on me. It was a grueling process that involved lots of travelling, reading and with no friend to lean on in the country.

During the hearings one of their witnesses, a former colleague, lectured me about how fair the company was to him and how everyone had a fair shot at what they wanted to be or do irrespective of where they hailed from. Because they had been fair to him, he thought they were fair to everyone. At that moment I wished that he could have walked in my shoes and experienced what I had. I was not asking for favours or special treatment but simply to be treated fairly. It was not meant to be such a lofty ideal.

The unsavoury character talked about how he had some sort of values and would never have done what I alleged. Whose word would they believe?

They contrived to diminish and disparage what I had done in the company for about six years. With the masks now off, I saw them for what they really were.

While the case was in progress, they decided to send me the final salary which they had withheld when I left. I took it but refused to crawl under a rock.

Long into the process, I had come to the realization that this was just one little battle. The war involved the rest of society, that society. The allegations of racist abuse were thrown out because of a statutory limitation on time. My abusers had, I am sure had long moved on way before that.

My lawyers ran the case in such a way that it was hard to tell if they were actually trying to win it. The preparation was rushed, at times changing critical aspects on the day, minutes before the hearing. They were the experts, but were they doing this right? They whittled down the number of comparators from over ten to one. They appeared incompetent at best, or working for the other side at worst.

I did not take the decision to go to the tribunal lightly, but a semblance of fairness and a glimmer of hope that justice might prevail spurred me on. One part of my evidence involved the salary discussion (a small part of which had been recorded) I had with my then manager. The tribunal chose to believe their version of events. Their defense to the fact that the other person had been performing the same duties but was less qualified and certified, but paid much more was that he had worked there for a longer time and was "more socially competent." Again the tribunal took their assertion as a convincing defense for the glaring disparity in salaries.

It was a triple whammy of devastating uppercuts. Was it a draw or a loss?

I was unhappy with the verdict in which only partial consideration had been given to my evidence. Was that the sound of a champagne bottle being popped open?

In the end, the outcome was a rewriting of the famous biblical story. Goliath had won. Little David had been swatted. I did not appeal the ruling. By now, I was exhausted. Physically, mentally, emotionally and financially. It was now time to crawl under that rock.

I was satisfied that I had challenged what I saw to be an injustice even though the odds were heavily stacked against me. A sense of fairness had eluded me. However, through the case some of the practices, the organisation of the institutions meant to redress such practices, and their associated procedures had been brought out into the light of day.

To better understand how something works, the gears and levers that make it tick, the inherent biases or imbalances, you need to open it, climb on it, get inside it, or even go under it. I had gone through the system. That system glossed over my evidence, skimmed over some facts, declared them more credible than me and inevitably came to the wrong or a foregone conclusion. I would have been more accepting of any outcome had it been even handed. But as matters stood, the whole thing had been a waste of my money and time.

Chapter 11

This Happened Because…

One evening a politician out canvassing for votes knocked on my door. He shook my hand, thrust a flyer in my face, said a few sweet words and was about to fly off when I stopped him. I told him about my issues and asked him how they could be put on his agenda. His face momentarily clouded with confusion and he then he literally just flew off.

My late grandmother had never seen the inside of a classroom. Only in her old age did she venture outside her village. She had also never met a White person until much later when White people went to her village. As was usual, if not always the case, it started with the missionaries.

They set up a missionary station in a remote village not too far from my granny's village. They built a Church, a small school and a nice house for the priests. Then they set about the business of evangelising and converting the heathen natives.

The area they picked was rumoured to have emeralds, real emeralds. The missionaries seemed to choose the remotest of remote places to establish their bases. Most of those places had precious stones. Someone made a passing remark about how this was such a strange coincidence.

Anyhow, the missionaries changed the natives' names and started to discourage their pagan practices and customs.

Twice a week in a village close to granny's, the natives would hold a dance they called "Sundown". It started late in the afternoon and rambled on until late in the evening. They would sing, dance and play drums and other musical instruments. This was accompanied by drinking and being merry. The priest visited the village during some of those "Sundowns". He never participated. He never went native. On the contrary, he deemed it unchristian. It also used to disturb his afternoon siesta as you could hear the music from miles away.

Therefore one evening he set about dismantling this pagan practice once and for all. He went to the venue of the Sundown and asked for "the drum that brings out the dance."

He went round testing the drums one by one. He would hit one and say: "No, this is not the drum that brings out the dance." Then he moved on to the next one until he came to a big and loud drum.

He hit it with his hand, and listened.

"Aaah! This is the drum that brings out the dance!"

To the natives' horror, he whipped out an axe and smashed the drum to pieces.

The natives beat him up.

The priest was so indignant that he cursed that village, telling them that "no one will ever go beyond primary school in that village."

Up to this day, there were very few people who had gone beyond primary school in that village because, apparently the curse bad worked, it had persisted. That was how granny concluded her story.

She neglected to mention the fact that there were no emeralds in that village, successive local governments had ignored the area and for some reason the missionaries had neither pitched their base nor built a school there, unlike in the other village which had emeralds. Whoever had made it beyond primary school had to walk long distances to get to the higher school.

However, I can say definitively that I did not hear a single racist word escape her mouth. I did not hear a single racial epithet from the people of that village. On the contrary, they extended a very warm welcome to White people who visited. They welcomed priests who went there to celebrate mass with arms open wide. Why did she or they not harbour any racial hatred?

As a matter of fact I visited a number of villages with White people on a number of occasions. I neither saw them subjected to humiliation because of the colour of their skin nor did any complain about such treatment. On the contrary, they were feted. Hold on, I did hear one complaint when we visited a restaurant. We were presented with menus that included local dishes whilst the White man only got some familiar western food. He wanted to have a taste of the local cuisine!

I was privileged to meet some genuine, really good people in Ireland. But I also found a lot of nasty people. "There were only a few bad eggs, one rotten tomato." They would say, or "to just ignore them." I was told. Those were the few explanations I could elicit from discussions with Irish friends and colleagues. My experiences pointed to the opposite. It was the other way round. I met a few nice people and a lot of really bad ones. It was the good people who were in the minority. How was that possible?

Then I sought my own answers. Anything to make me understand! Some opined that racism was due to ignorance. It was due to a lack of education others said. We were never a colonial power, we were colonized too. Well, this is their racism, I thought. There was this need to want to hastily "move on", or for the victim "to become thicker skinned" to such abuse without necessarily addressing the underlying causes or issues.

The potato famine took place a long time ago. But I heard about it a lot. About how it had exposed the mean streak in the English psyche. They still remembered. The English were never spared. They were loathed and abused for this and many other crimes they were accused of. It all happened a long time ago. Why had they not forgotten?

The intensity of the hatred was mind boggling, the hostility unrelenting. It spanned a wide spectrum as well, from the crude gutter and ignorant type, to the subtle, arrogant and condescending type. Kids, women, girls, boys, old men and old women, everyone piled on. On the road, in the house, in the pub, at work, in church, on the bus, at university, in a public toilet, in the park, on the train, in a café, hotel, restaurant, in the airport, at a funeral, everywhere! How could this be?

If I complained I was playing the race card, or trying to impose political correctness, or even stifling their freedom to abuse me. They had all sorts of arguments to support their freedom to threaten, insult and humiliate me. Was it me I asked myself? Would this mindset exist if I had not come here?

I tried to ignore them, confront them, talk to them, reason with them, be nice to them, buy them a pint, laugh with them, engage or embarrass them. I went as far as praying for them. You know, praying for our enemies and turning the other cheek? Nothing worked. The hatred seemed pathological. I did not even need to be there to be reviled.

"This is new to us. We are an island nation. We are not used to immigration."

But then why tell me about how the Irish had travelled far and wide, themselves being well accepted and lauded or badly mistreated. Had they not learnt anything from that?

In spite of all that I had experienced during the time I spent in Ireland, I never ever met a person who admitted to holding racist views. No one admitted to having done, said, or propagated racial bigotry. I never heard anyone admit to discriminating against people or showing any intolerance on racial grounds. Even with all the Catholic, Protestant, Royalist, and Republican sectarianism, the only side I ever heard from was the victim's. The perpetrator remained silent, or hidden.

People have been killed because of what or who they are. I only bear the mental, emotional, psychological, physical, and economic scars. The traumas had taken their toll. It was time to seek out that exit.

A president and an opposition politician were having an argument in a different country. One of them began losing the political argument. Putting aside his esteemed status in society he chose to muddy the water instead. He somehow injected into the discussion how the other smoked an illegal substance. This was roundly and strongly denied by the president. The opposition politician made a telling observation before going quiet "If you want to know how the crocodile lives, ask the hippo."

If you want to know about the one hundred thousand welcomes, talk to someone who has been treated to those welcomes.

Chapter 12

Which Way My Child?

This is my story and these are my perceptions. No one will speak for me nor will my experiences remain a statistic. Even though I have no knowledge about what prison feels like (I do not intend to find out), I felt like I had just left prison having served a sentence for the crime of being Black. I would never wish the horrible experiences I went through on anybody else. I wish I could reach inside my head, with my bare hands and rip out the terrible memories. If only the positive memories could dilute the impact of the insults.

My prayer is that my children do not experience what I underwent anywhere in the world. I now understand what prompted my ancestors to fight for independence and why it should be celebrated. I have faith but I am short on optimism.

When I talked to other non-National colleagues, I found that their stories resonated with mine and others'. They were not isolated as others would have me believe. If anything they appeared systematic, coordinated by an evil something. Only extreme instances would bubble up to the top of the political or media agenda. They would usually be in the form of a brief headline here or a buried filler story there. There was no empathy, no sympathy, and most importantly no plan to confront the issues. The low level incidences fashioned to make people like myself really uncomfortable were met with silence followed by selective amnesia. I did not wish to stay silent because then I would be just as culpable as the perpetrators.

Poland had only recently joined the EU. As is usual it begun to receive a massive inflow of EU funding. Multinationals followed suit. Its economy was on the upswing. Construction started to pick up.

There were jobs to be had. Some Polish nationals started heading back home.

Some Irish people started making their way to Poland in search of work as well. The roles had been reversed. Unfortunately stories about how the Polish had been treated on construction sites in Ireland had filtered back to Poland. It was payback time. This is not to say Poland itself had an impeccable reputation with regard to race relations.

I was disturbed but not surprised to see headlines such as "'No Irish' builders sought on Polish sites" staring back at me from the pages of the Irish Times and other dailies. Ironically, this particular headline was placed right next to another one urging Ahern (the minister in charge of immigration) not to deport a Serbian family from Ireland.

"No Irish" signs were apparently being put up on Polish construction sites. I had read about similar signs being used in the UK a while back. It was not a pretty sight. Someone in Poland had thought it appropriate to import the same discriminatory and humiliating signs. I wondered whether they too did not learn anything from what they had gone through.

These things did not happen during medieval times, or in a lawless backwater tribal enclave. It happened in the 21st Century, in first world countries at the forefront of modern civilisation.

There were no elephants, lions or buffaloes being shot. There was no going native or being attended to by armies of servants. I was neither on holiday nor did I come to exploit anybody. It was only hard work, high hopes and belief. The expectations were quickly and comprehensively dashed and replaced by disillusionment and cynicism.

Be prepared. My sincere hope is that you will have a much better experience.

I do not know where Ireland will end up with regard to racial and cultural harmony. I do not know what these parents are teaching those children so that those future adults will know what to do.

For me the road had at first glance looked well paved and smooth, with a few hills and valleys as one would expect, but promising. The barriers erected by human hands had confined me to that one narrow road, and it became narrower with each step. As I went further down the road, clouds had gathered, the sky turned grey and gradually turned into a storm. There was nothing beyond those hills. However, there was something very valuable along the way. I had reached the end of the road. It culminated in a dead drop, a steep cliff. I had been on a road to nowhere all along.

I have no idea how Ireland will deal with the reality of its modern racial and cultural make-up. I guess they will find out in a generation what today's parents are teaching their children.

The happy ending to this story will come when the story ends.

A Few Definitions

The Pale - A wall that surrounded Dublin a long time ago. It still exists, only metaphorically these days. At times it could also surround minds.

Garda Síochána - Irish Police

TD –Irish for MP

Taoiseach – Irish Prime Minister

Fianna Fáil – An Irish political party

Fine Gael – Another Irish political party (I couldn't tell the difference either)

A & E – Accident and Emergency

Craic – Having fun, usually fueled by lots of alcohol

Bodhran – a drum cut in two to make two half drums that can be played separately, seemingly.

Unfàilte - a made up word meaning the opposite of fàilte.

Further Reading

1. The party is definitely over, The Economist, Mar 19th 2009

2. Skills shortage may force Openet to seek 50 software staff abroad,
   http://www.irishtimes.com/newspaper/finance/2012/06 14/1224317871488.html

3. Skills shortages can be addressed,
   http://www.irishtimes.com/newspaper/education/2011/1220/1224309289199.html

4. Central Statistics Office - Crime and Justice,
   http://www.cso.ie/en/statistics/crimeandjustice/

5. National Development Plan 2007-2013, The Stationery Office (Government Publications Sale Office)

6. Housing slump in Ireland continues,
   http://www.globalpropertyguide.com/Europe/Ireland/Price-History

7. Gerry Ryan 1956-2010 ,
   http://www.irishexaminer.com/ireland/kfkfidqlcwau/rss2/ ,10 Mar 2012

8. Gerry Ryan on life, love and death,
   http://www.independent.ie/lifestyle/independent-woman/celebrity-news-gossip/gerry-ryan-on-life-love-and-death-2161826.html, 2 May 2010

9. Permanent TSB/ESRI House Price Index 1996 – 2011,
   http://www.esri.ie/irish_economy/permanent_tsbesri_house_p

10. Human, animal waste found in Galway water,
    http://www.rte.ie/news/2007/0328/water.html

11. Latest Water Update 20/08/2007,
    http://www.galway.ie/en/Services/WaterServices/Wate
    rContamination/Archives/
12. Ireland in the EU - Joining the European Comunity,
    http://ec.europa.eu/ireland/ireland_in_the_eu/index1_e
    n.htm
13. Deaths and injuries on Irish roads,
    http://www.rsa.ie/RSA/Road-Safety/Our-
    Research/Deaths-injuries-on-Irish-roads/
14. Welcome, http://www2.merriam-webster.com/cgi-
    bin/mwdictsn?book=Dictionary&va=welcome
15. Fàilte, http://en.wiktionary.org/wiki/fàilte
16. No Irish need apply: Polish builders get their own
    back, http://www.belfasttelegraph.co.uk/news/local-
    national/no-irish-need-apply-polish-builders-get-their-
    own-back-14126902.html#ixzz25IXWuuDM
17. M50 Gypsies abandon Irish dream,
    http://www.guardian.co.uk/world/2007/jul/29/ireland
18. Anger at 'lazy' Roma remarks,
    http://www.independent.ie/national-news/anger-at-
    lazy-roma-remarks-1254883.html
19. Ireland deports Roma after stand-off over roundabout,
    http://www.independent.co.uk/news/world/europe/ire
    land-deports-roma-after-standoff-over-roundabout-
    458753.html
20. Northern Ireland: further racist attack against
    Romanians in Belfast,
    http://www.telegraph.co.uk/news/uknews/law-and-
    order/5565531/Northern-Ireland-further-racist-attack-
    against-Romanians-in-Belfast.html

21. Racist attacks timeline,
    http://news.bbc.co.uk/1/hi/northern_ireland/8104498.stm

22. Global Competitiveness,
    http://www.weforum.org/issues/global-competitiveness

23. Economic Survey of Ireland 2011,
    http://www.oecd.org/eco/economicsurveyofireland2011.htm

2340747R10068

Printed in Germany
by Amazon Distribution
GmbH, Leipzig